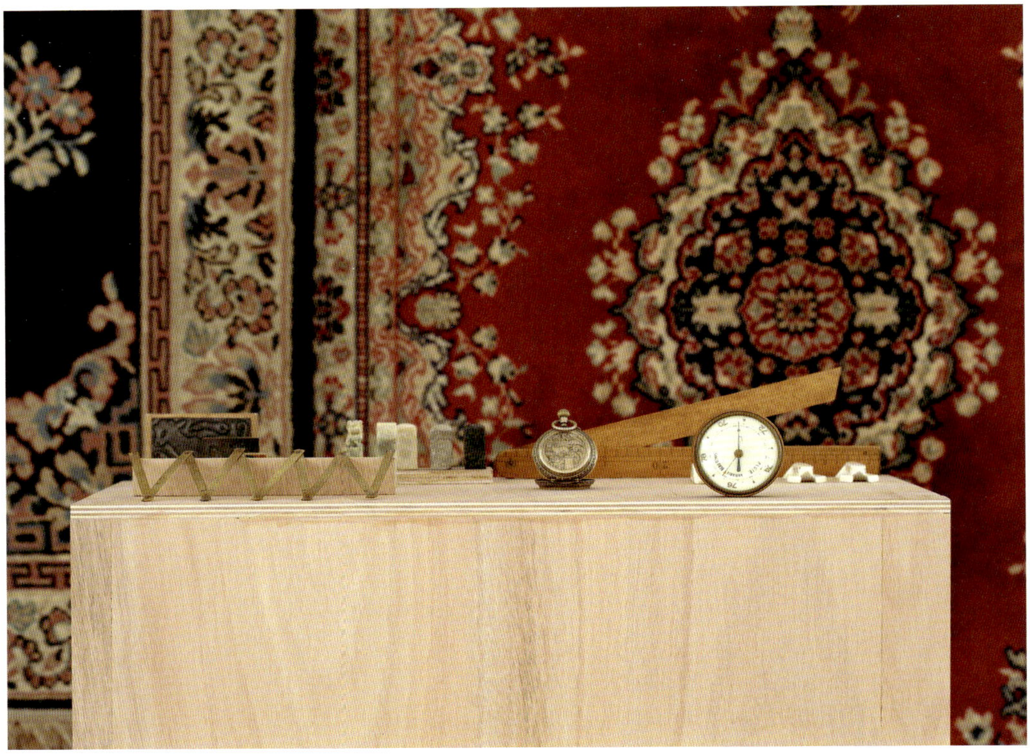

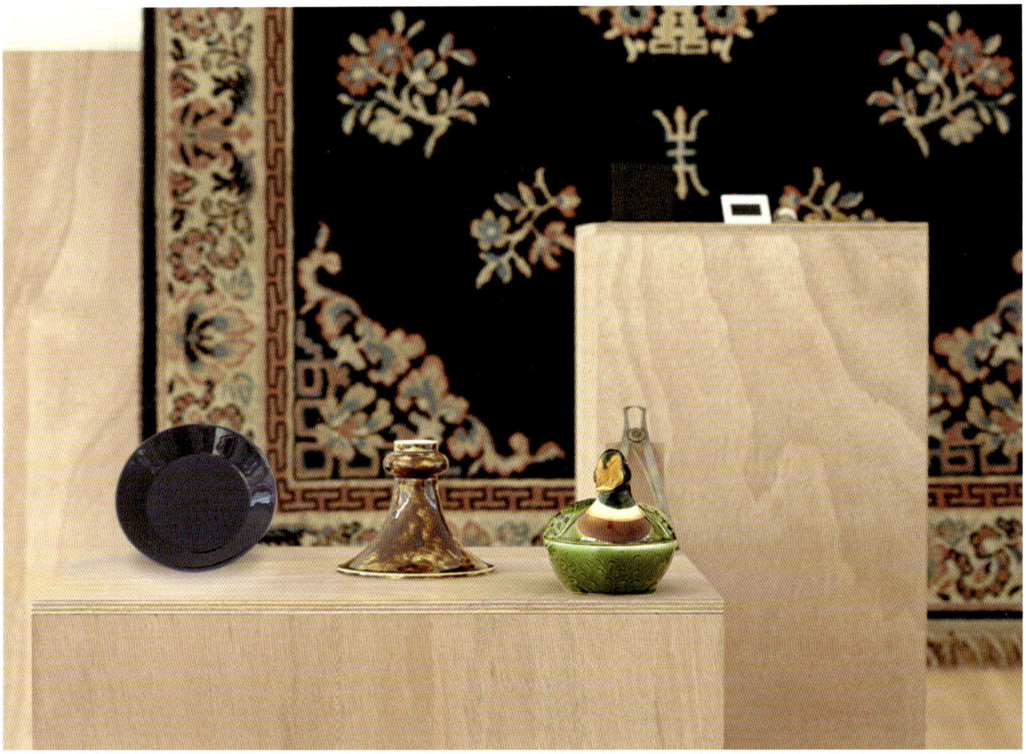

Paysage avec poussin et témoins oculaires (Version III), 2010 (details)

Vanishing Points and Emerging Forms
Vivian Sky Rehberg

The first, and perhaps most obvious, questions that arise when embarking on a writerly journey into Isabelle Cornaro's mixed media artistic production have to do with perspective, point of view, and position. Where and how do I situate myself (both figuratively and literally) with respect to the intricate and multilayered formal structure of her work as a whole, and in relation to the individual drawings, photographs and films, paintings, installations and sculptures that comprise it? Where do I stand, what do I privilege, and what will I necessarily, if inadvertently, neglect to notice at this particular juncture in her career?

Mulling over such concerns is not only a matter of course when writing about contemporary art. These are questions generated by Cornaro's specific materials, processes, and aesthetic approach to date, which oblige one to heed Yve-Alain Bois' claim that "concepts must be forged *from* the object of one's inquiry or be imported according to that object's specific exigency."[1] Bois' ideal critical method is especially relevant to Cornaro's work. As an object-centered outlook, it underscores an artwork's conditions of production, the conjunction of its material components and aesthetic properties, and its location in a field of continually proliferating objects. And, like Cornaro's artistic practice, it considers the position and place of the subjects, namely the artist and viewers, interacting with and within that field.[2]

1 Yve-Alain Bois, *Painting as Model*, MIT Press, Cambridge, Massachusetts, 1990, p. XII and XIX.

2 A comprehensive analysis of Isabelle Cornaro's staging of the relationship between the spectator and the artwork would require tracing the historicization and theorization of the place of the spectator in 20th- and 21st-century art, via the work of Michael Fried, Rosalind Krauss, and Jonathan Crary among others. That genealogy is beyond the scope of this essay.

With all this in mind, the most convenient place to depart from is Cornaro's installation *Paysage avec poussin et témoins oculaires* (*Landscape with Chick and Eye Witnesses*), of which there are currently four versions (made in 2008, 2010, and 2011). This series of installations can be seen as an aesthetic matrix, but not as the chronological or conceptual point of origin, from whence her ongoing engagement with the aesthetic and ideological features of systems of representation emerges distinctly. Taking as its referent classical pastoral landscape painting, best exemplified by the work of 17th-century artist Nicolas Poussin, each *Paysage avec poussin et témoins oculaires* reinterprets the two-dimensional surface of a picture into a spatial arrangement of ordinary plywood plinths upon which are placed different objects. In all versions, the installation is loosely organized according to the principle of linear perspective, with the foreground, middle ground, and background signaled by the increasing height of the plinths, the rapprochement of the plans, and the decreasing size of the objects as we move further into the composition. In the first three versions, imitation oriental carpets, which are rolled into tight cylinders placed parallel to the front edges of the plinths or fully unfurled beneath them like an ornate woven terrain, pace the eye as it travels through the scene. At the back of the installation more carpets, hung vertically alongside similarly-scaled wood panels, serve as the eye's final resting place.

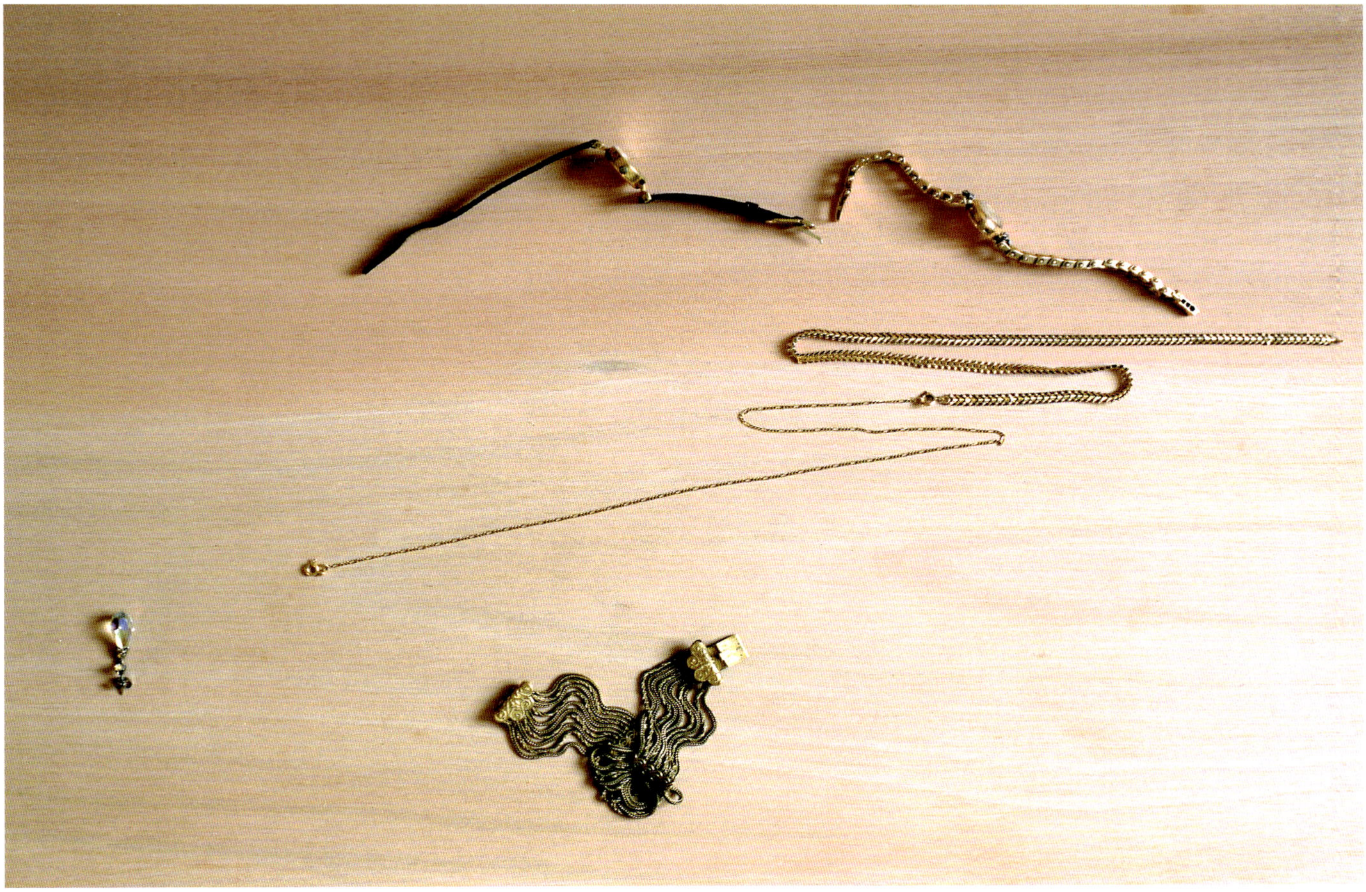

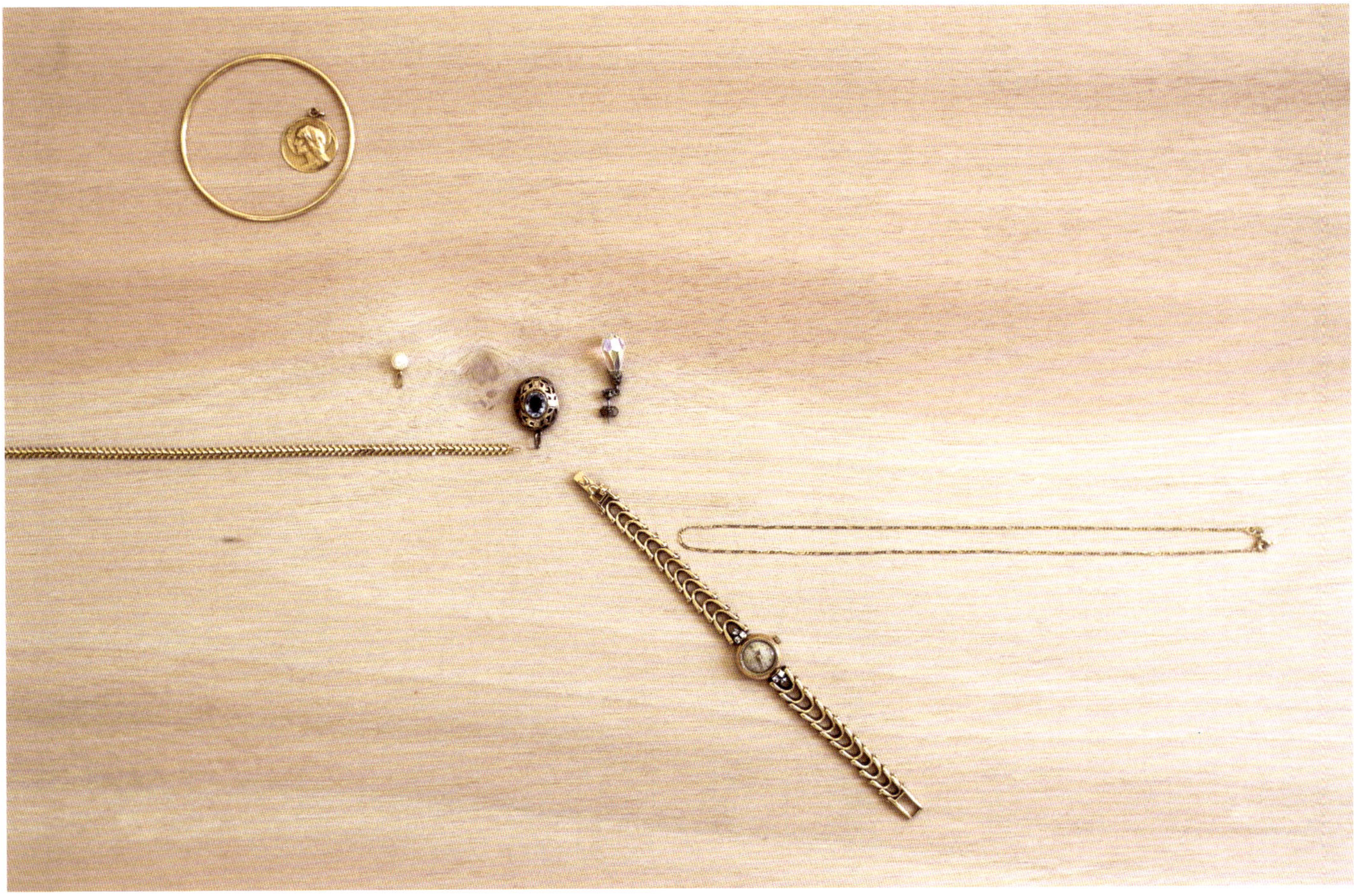

Savane autour de Bangui et le fleuve Utubangui, 2003–2007

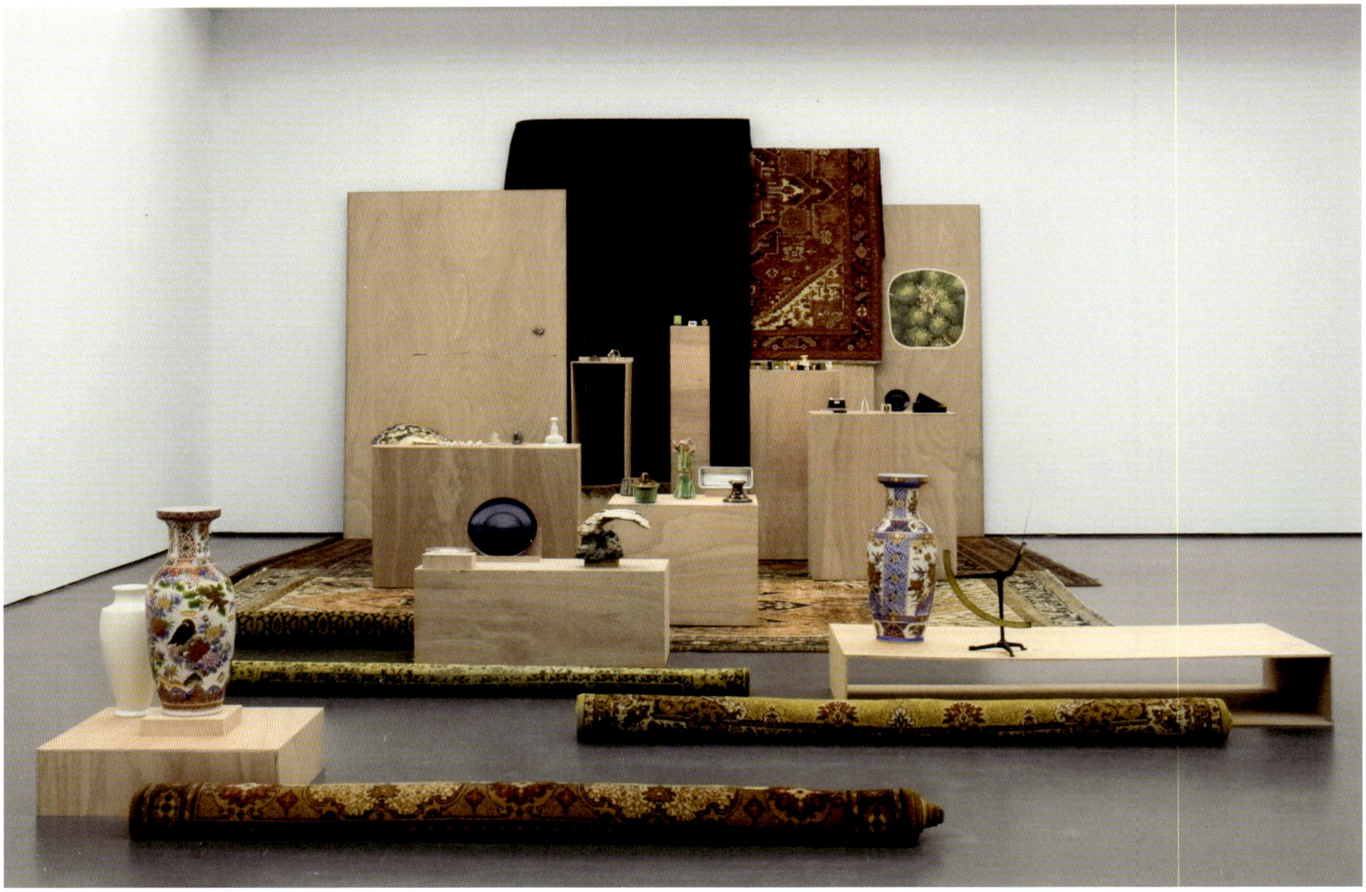

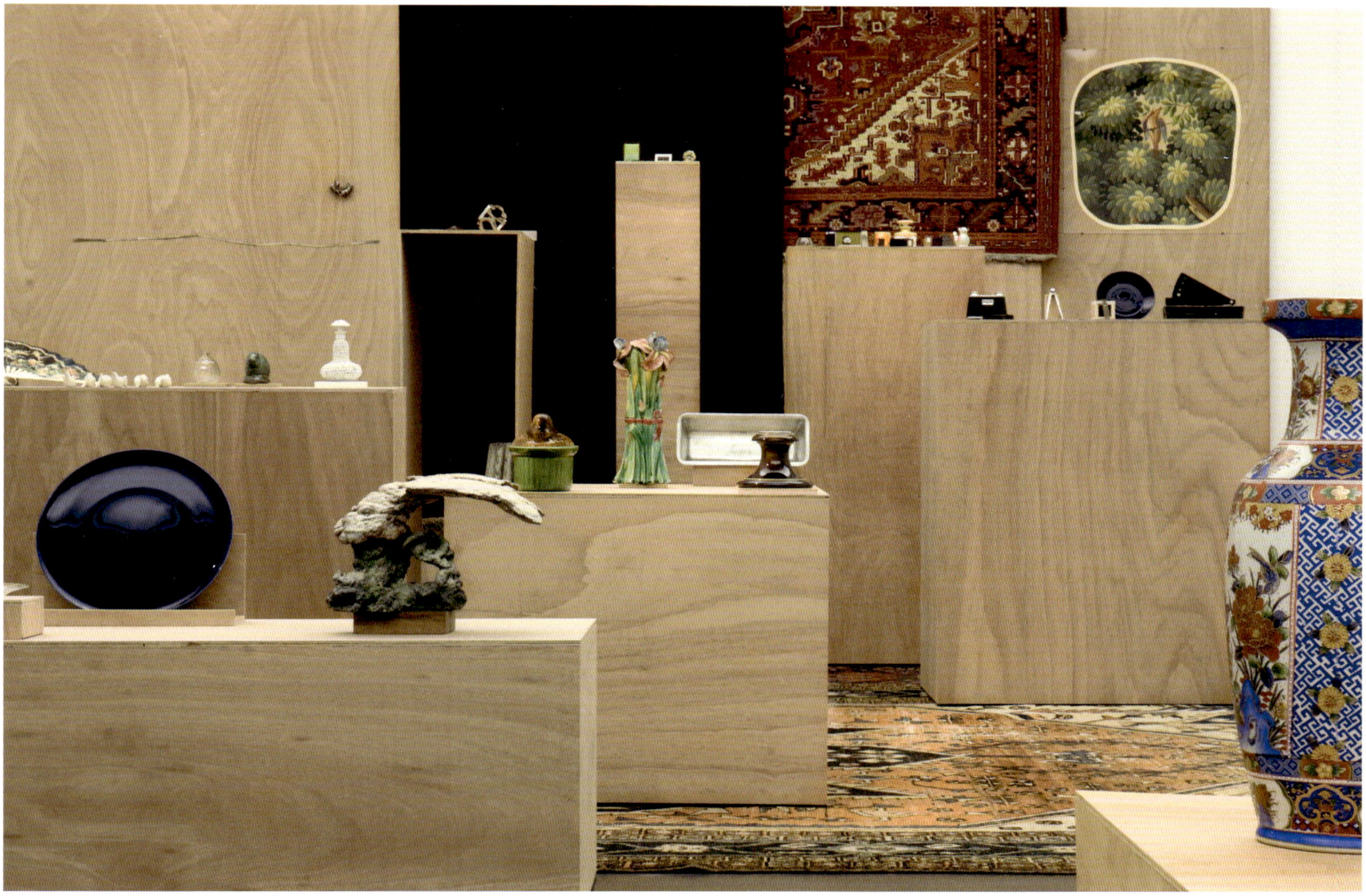

Paysage avec poussin et témoins oculaires (Version I), 2008

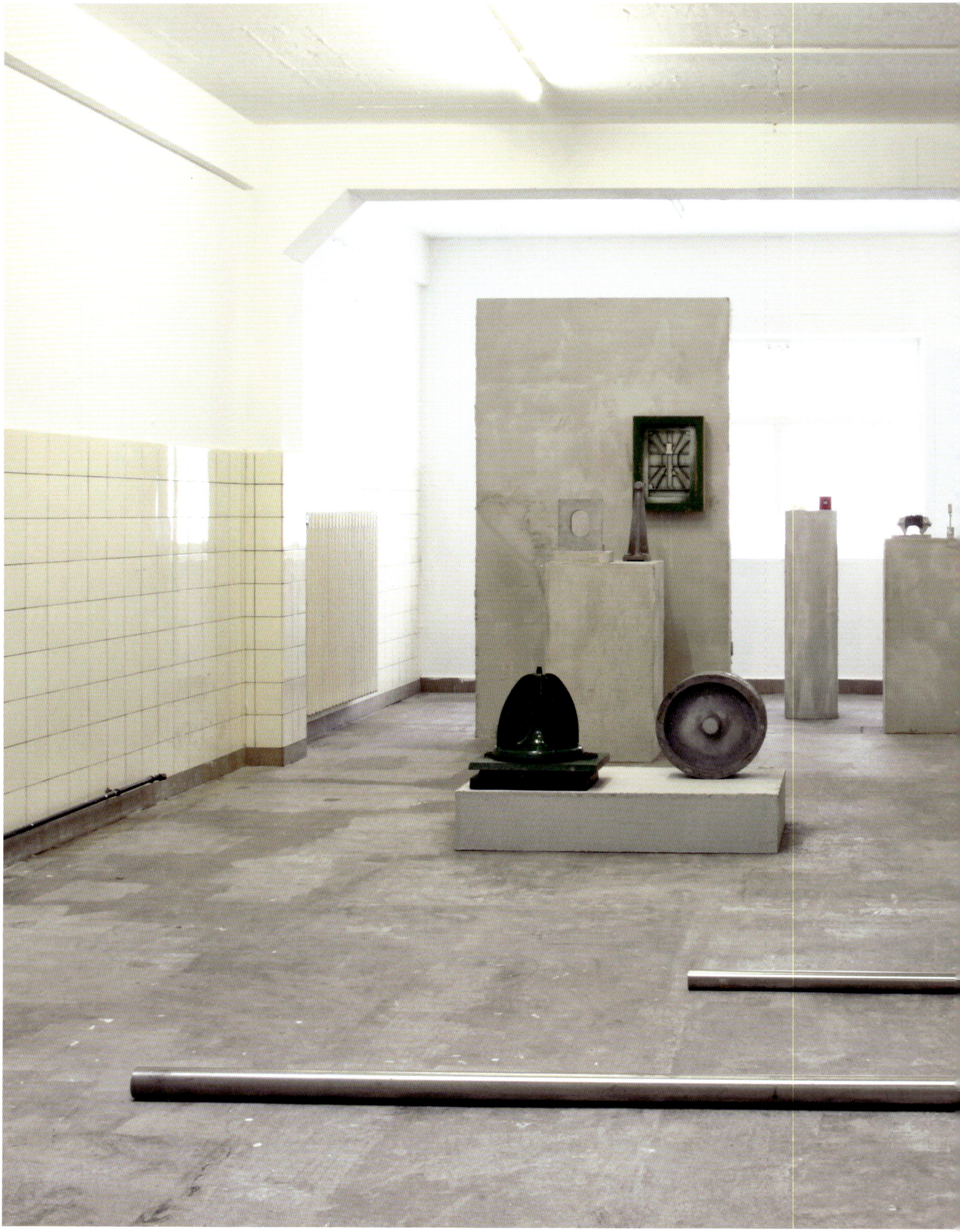

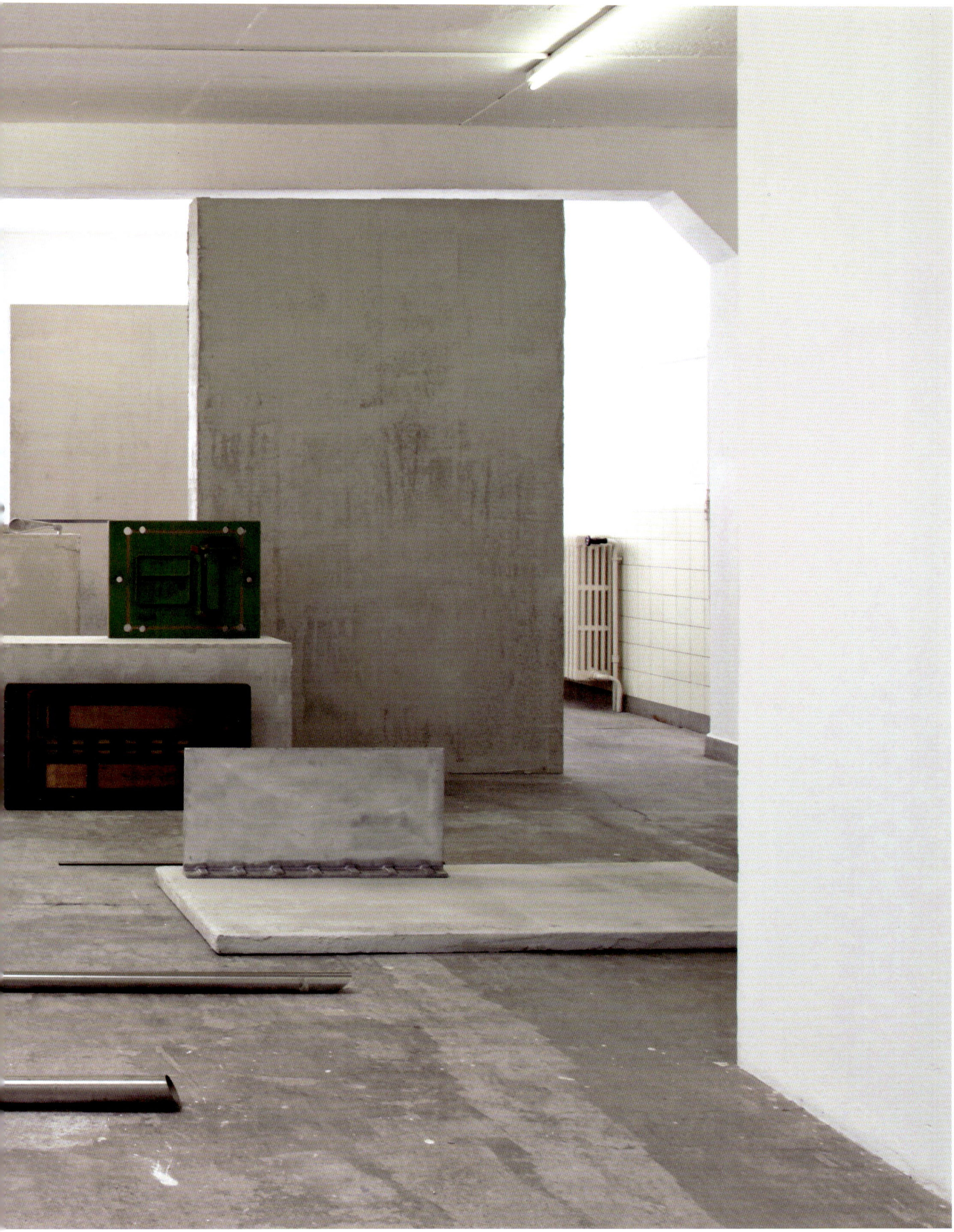

Paysage avec poussin et témoins oculaires (Version IV), 2011

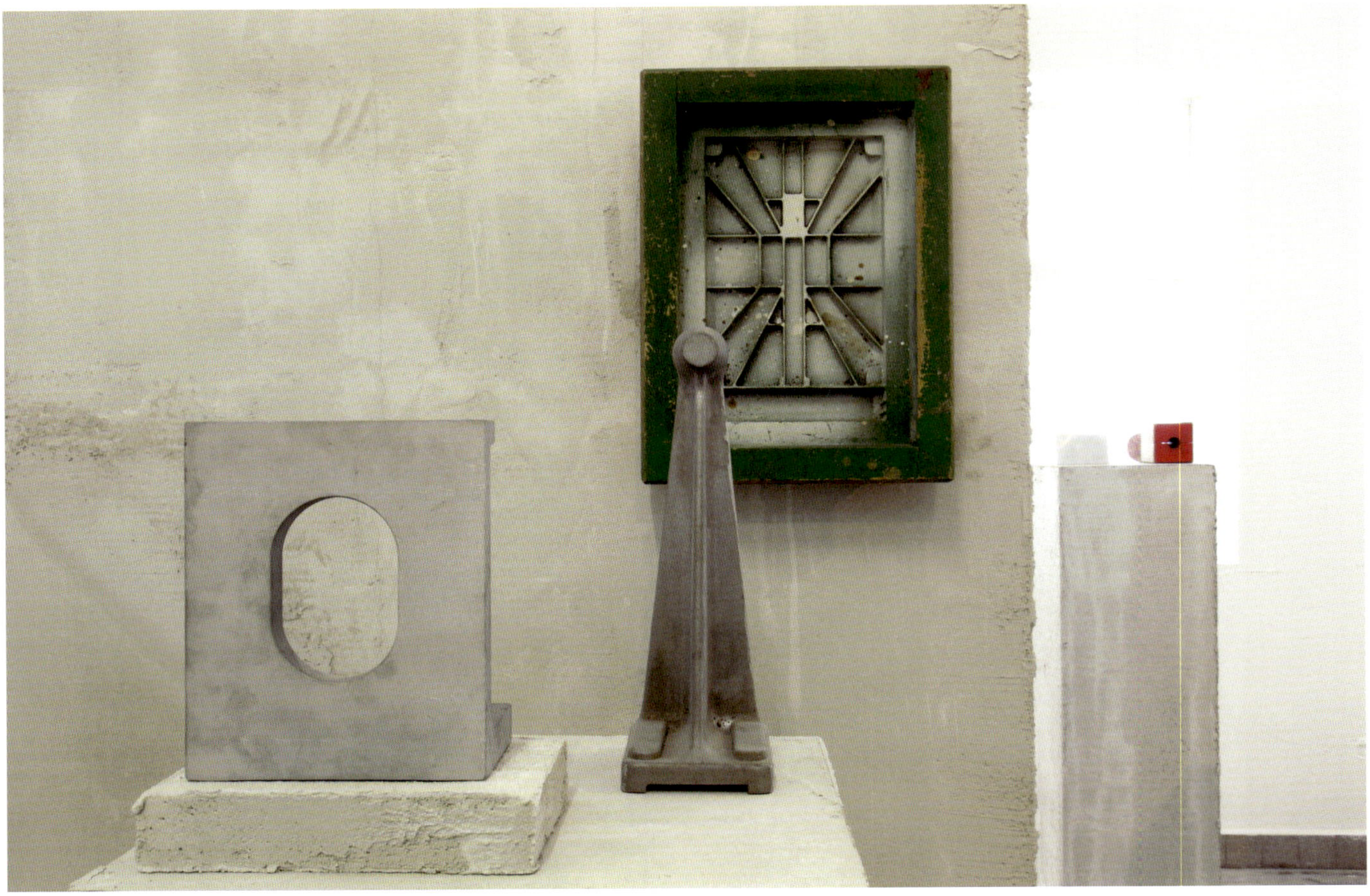

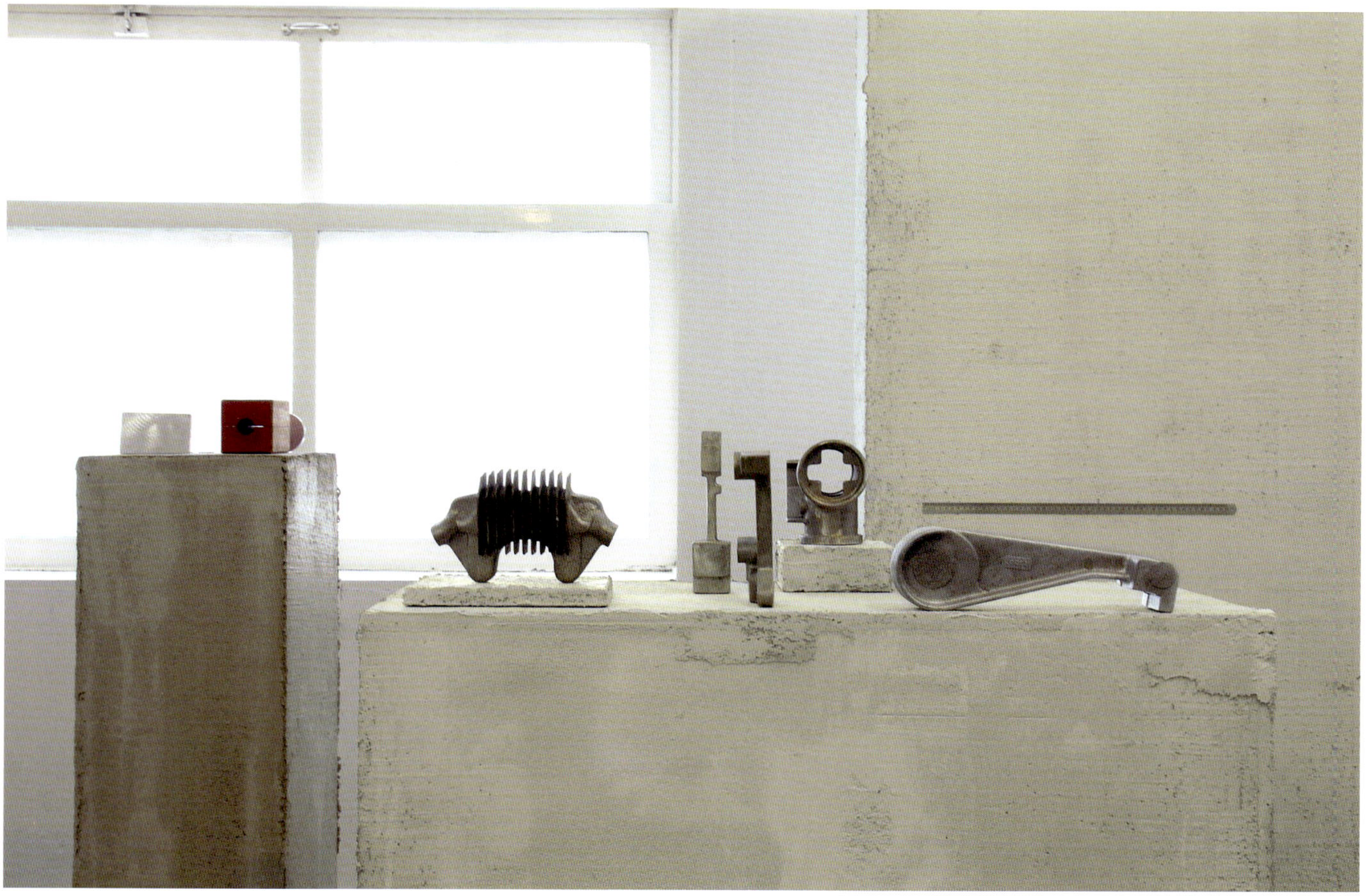

Paysage avec poussin et témoins oculaires (Version IV), 2011 (details)

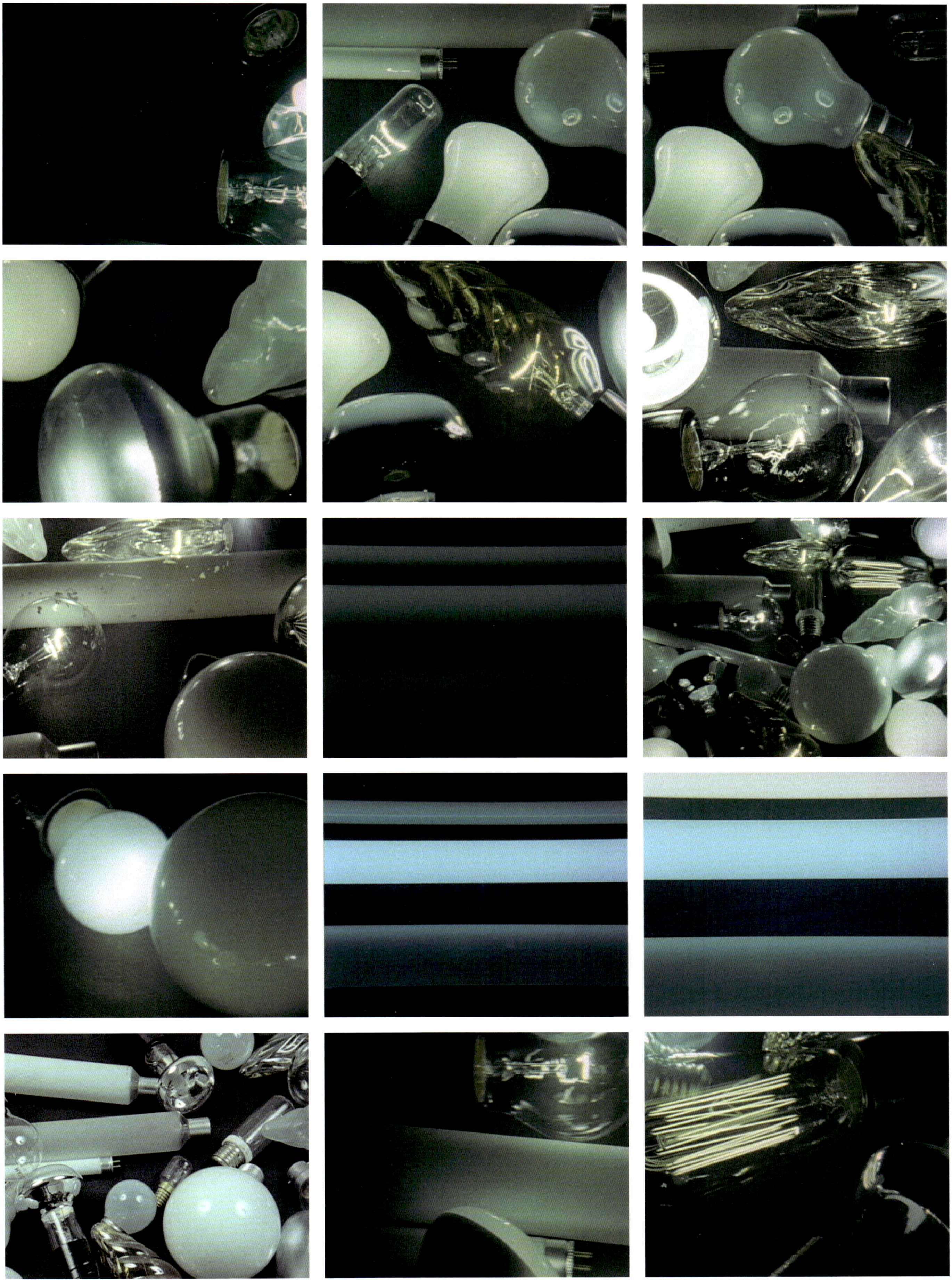

Film-Lampe, 2010

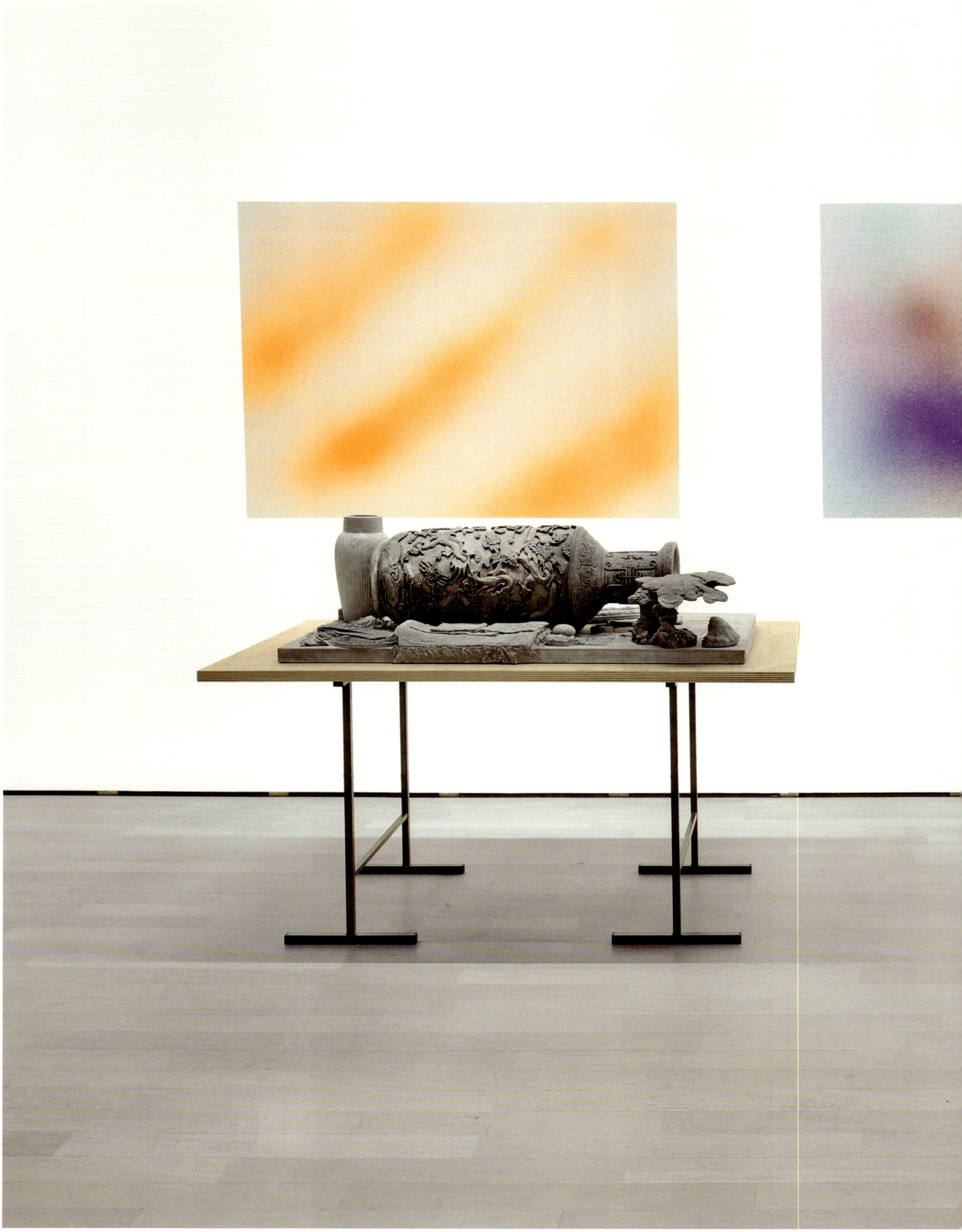

View of the exhibition *Monsieur Miroir*, Fondation d'Entreprise Ricard, Paris, 2010

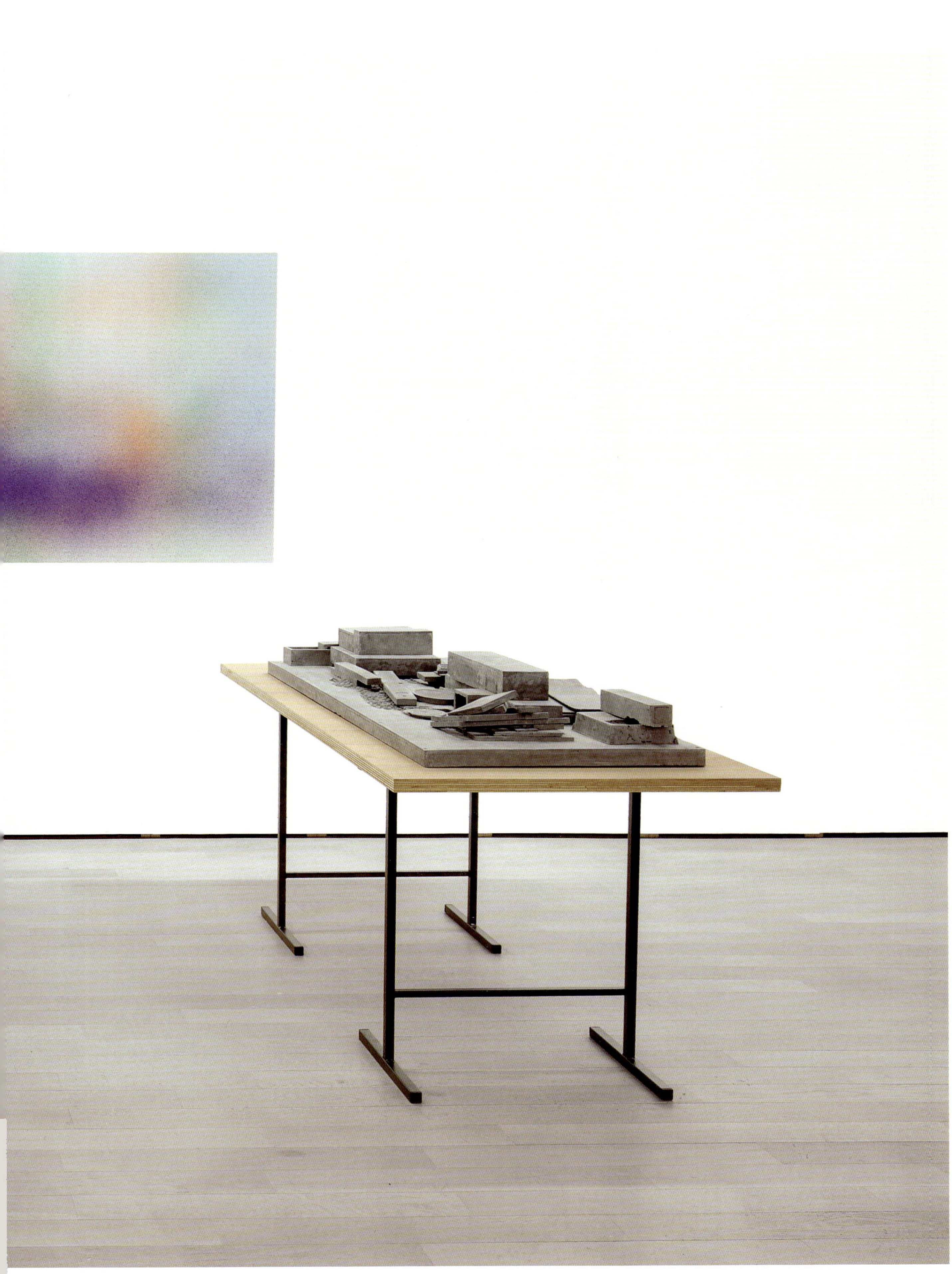

On the wall: *Impressions*, 2010; on the floor: *Homonymes*, 2010

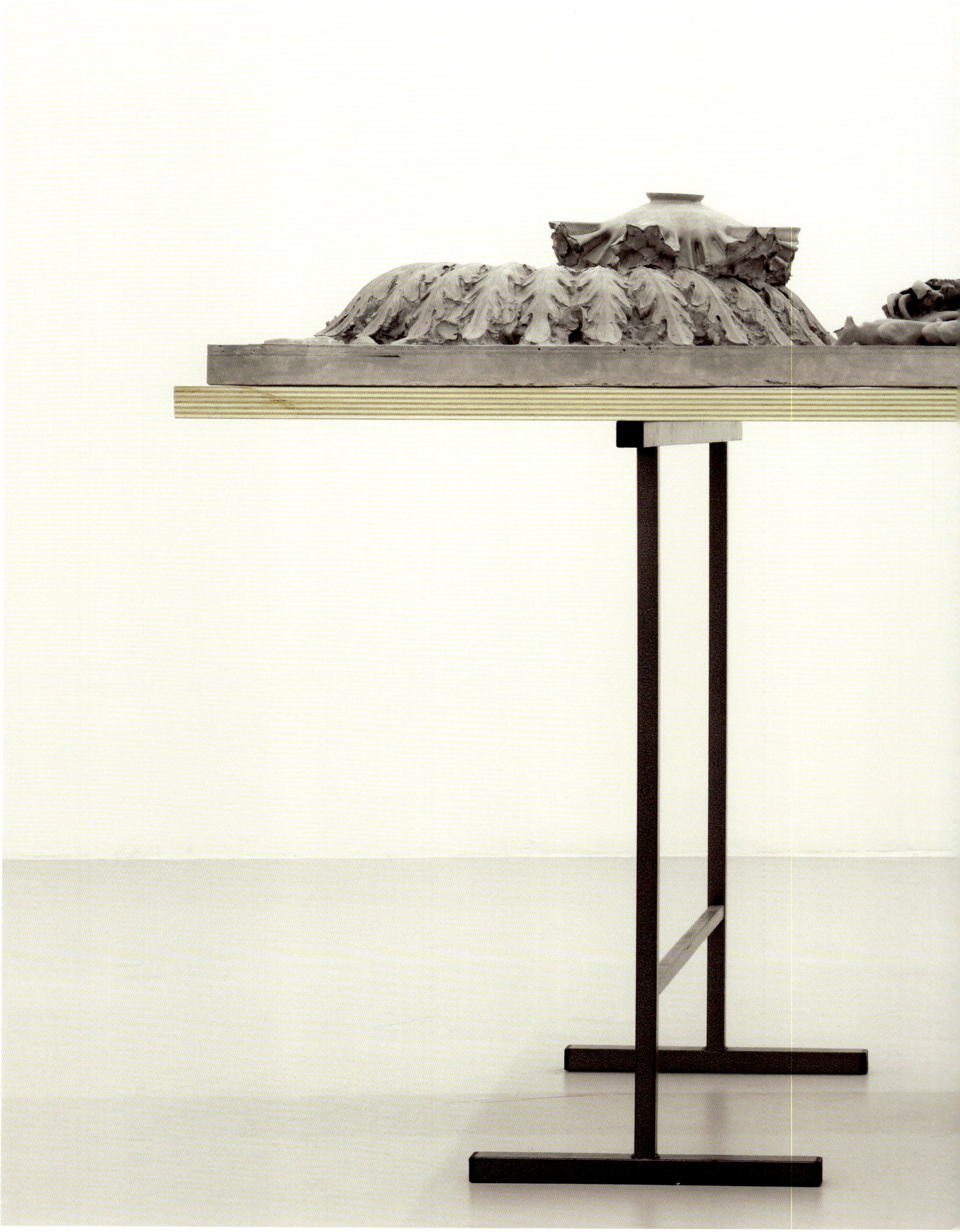

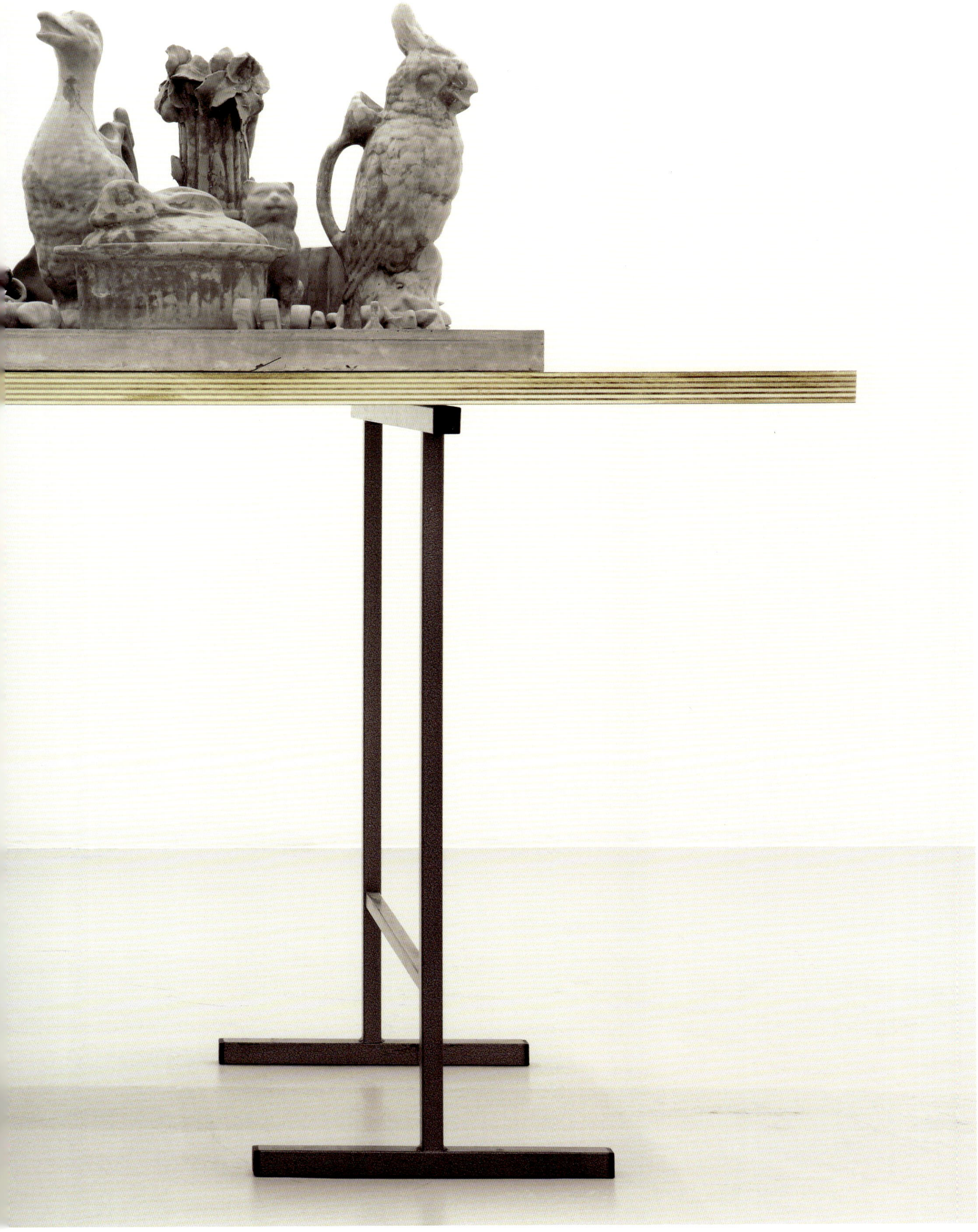

Homonymes, 2010

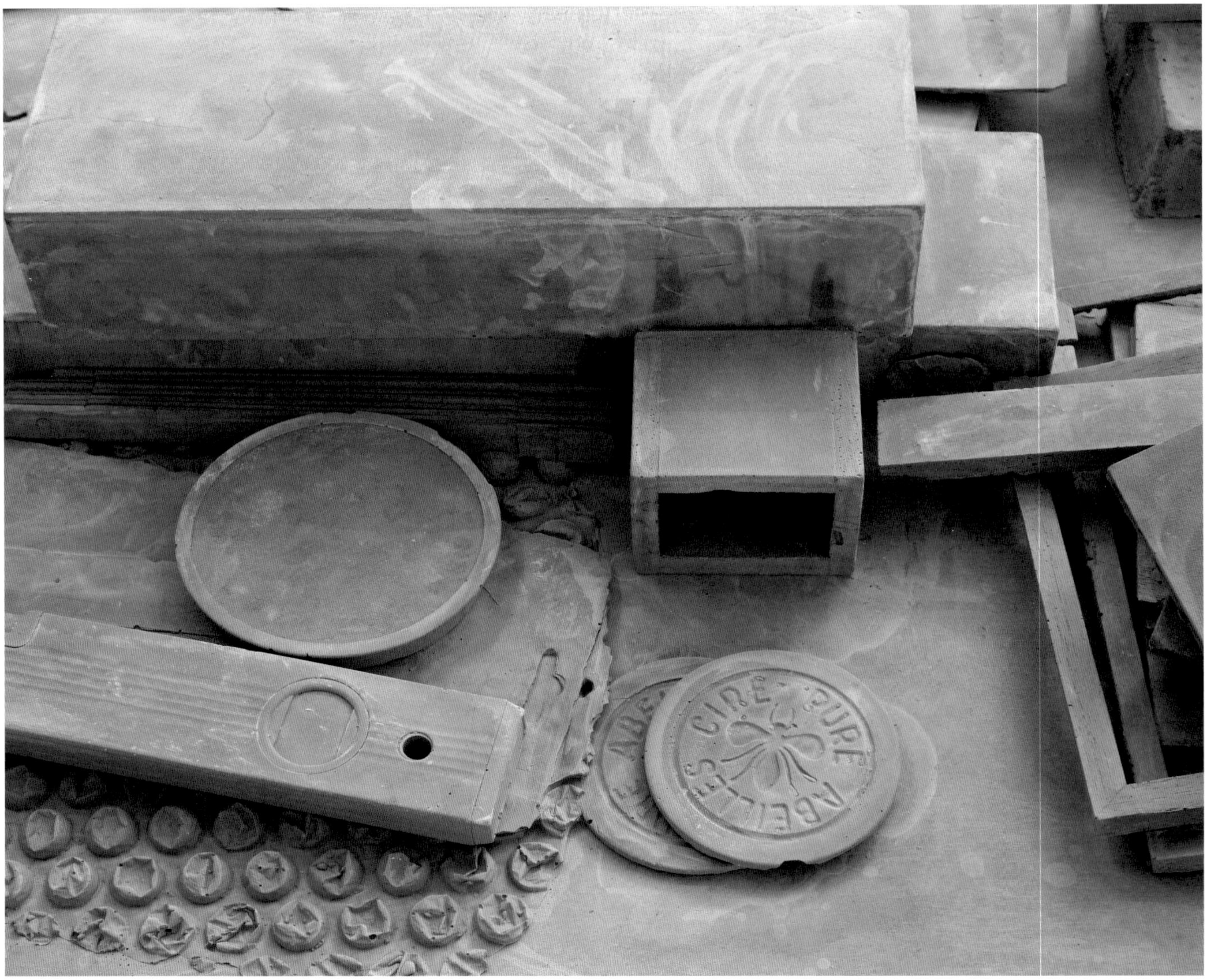

Homonymes, 2010 (detail)

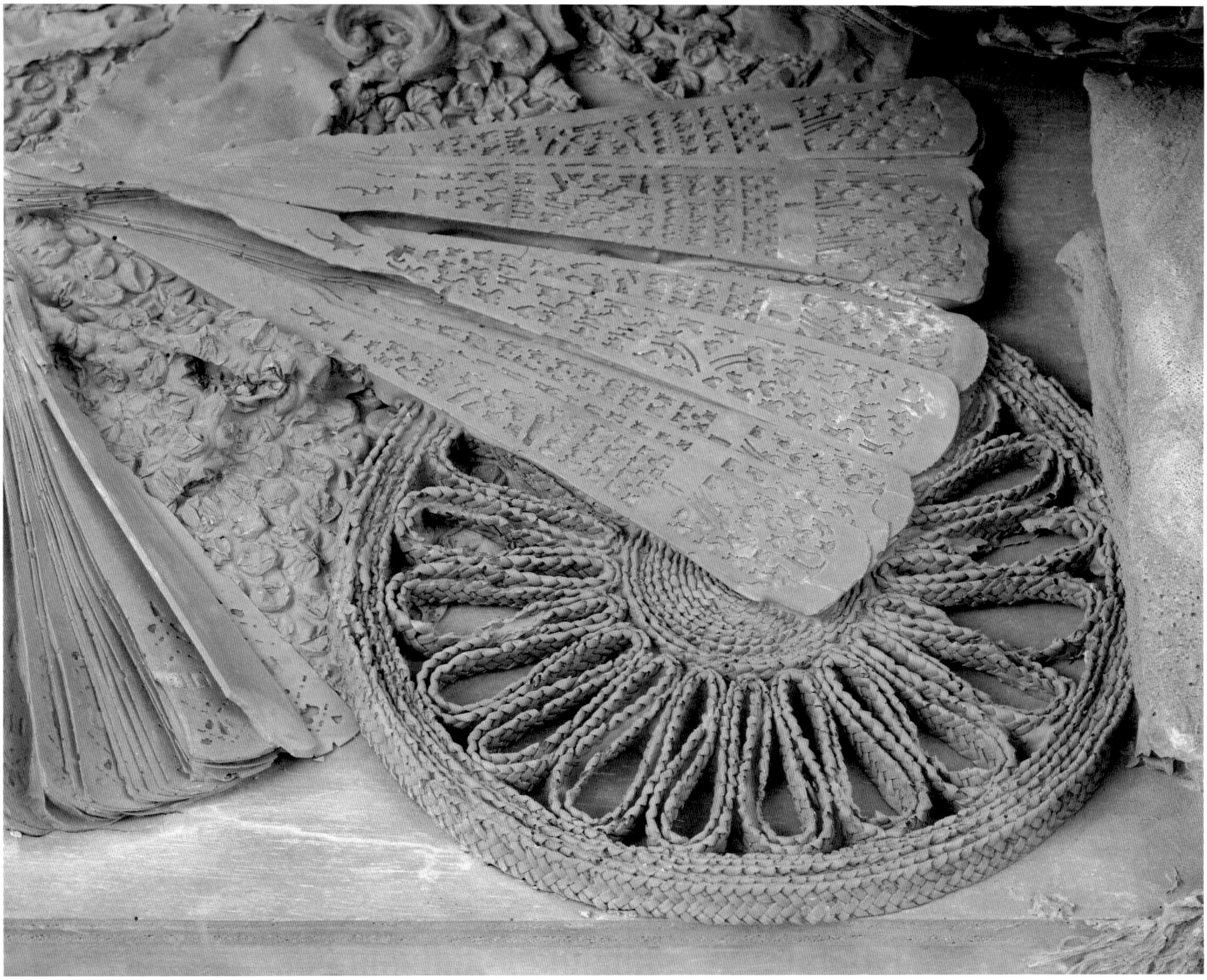

Homonymes, 2010 (detail)

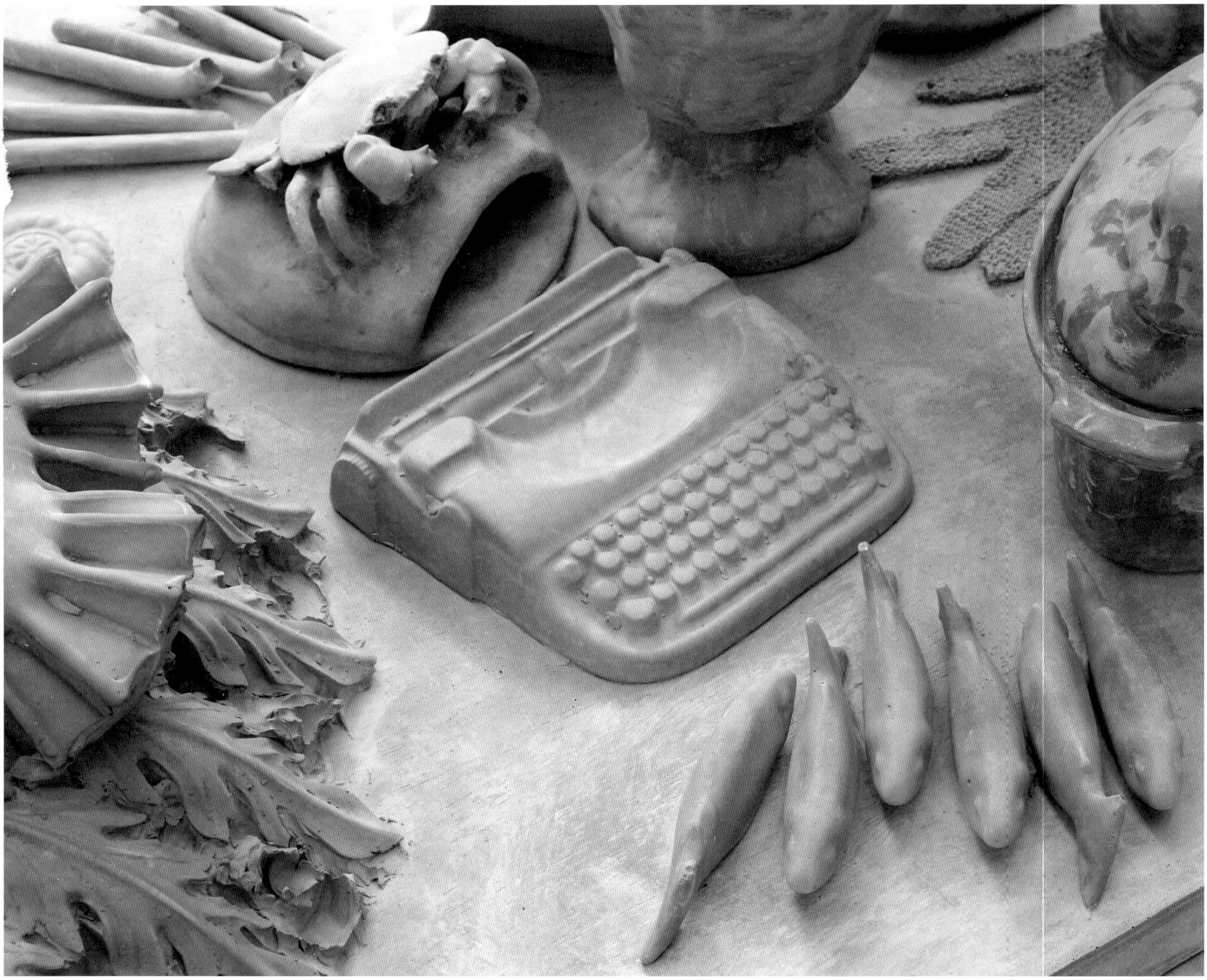

Homonymes, 2010 (detail)

Repointing: Isabelle Cornaro and the Index

Glenn Adamson

"Almost everyone is agreed about '70s art. It is diversified, split, factionalized."[1] These are the opening lines of Rosalind Krauss' celebrated two-part essay *Notes on the Index*, first published in *October* in 1977. The article was immediately influential, and became even more so when it was installed as a centerpiece of Krauss' *The Originality of the Avant Garde and Other Modernist Myths*, in 1985. What animated Krauss' essay was her idea that the index might be the rudder to steer us through a storm of indiscriminate art. As she explained, an index (as discussed in the work of Charles Peirce and other semioticians) is a sign that is linked to its referent through physical rather than conventional means—like a footprint in sand, a shadow, or a photograph. In each case there is an objective, direct construction of meaning. Gesturing to a tree, or taking its picture, is different from uttering the word "tree" because it cannot be transposed into another method of signification (as one might translate "tree" into "arbre" or "baum"). The index, she wrote, "substitute[s] the registration of sheer physical presence for the more highly articulated language of aesthetic conventions (and the kind of history which they encode)."[2]

1 Rosalind Krauss, "Notes on the Index, Part One," *October* 3 (Spring 1977), p. 68.

2 Krauss, "Notes on the Index," p. 81.

Let us not forget that 1977 was a moment primed for stylistic explosion. The formal/conceptual tradition of art theory, which informed Krauss' work and was in turn formed by it, was about to enter into all-out warfare with the heterogeneous welter of art styles we now call postmodernism. Facing this coming eclecticism, and the collapse of theoretical rigor that it portended, Krauss saw the "sheer physical presence" of the index as a stable foundation. It is no coincidence that 1977 also saw the multi-media exhibition *Pictures* open in New York, which initiated a surprising leapfrog of image reproduction from the backwaters of art history to its front lines, leading to a widespread reevaluation of photography in particular. For Krauss and her intellectual allies, the indexicality of the photograph (and the film, its time-and-animated based extension) would serve well into the 1980s as a bulwark against an increasingly miscellaneous art world.

Of course, if art was diversified, split, and factionalized in the 1970s, today it is positively atomized. Krauss' ambition was to keep alive the sense, propagated by Clement Greenberg and others at mid-century, that "advanced" art operated within a single discursive field, anchored in the concept of medium. From the perspective of 2011, this perhaps seems a quaint notion. Postmodernism and globalism may not have delivered on many of the freedoms they promised, but they achieved this much, anyway: an art world of complete mutual unintelligibility, of heteroglossia. As Mary Ann Doane points out in her discussion of this "post-medium condition," even the indexicality of photography itself has come to seem treacherous, as "the digital offers an ease of manipulation and distance from any referential grounding."[3]

3 Mary Ann Doane, "Indexicality: Trace and Sign: Introduction," *Differences* 18/1 (2007), p. 1.

Even in an art world of infinite diversity, however, certain common grounds do remain. One of these is the market—which sets the terms of engagement much as the abstraction vs. figuration debate did in the 1950s. A lesser-theorized, indeed often obscured, source of debate is artistic production itself. I often think, walking through any large-scale biennial or other international exhibition with a bewildering diversity of offerings, that a good way to assess all the works on view objectively is to think about how they were made. What we have in art today, mostly, are found objects, outsourced fabrication, "bad painting," videos, big photos printed on expensive equipment, "relational" situations requiring only rudimentary props, and outsized sloppy sculpture. Skilled hands are in evidence, but only very rarely are they the artist's own. One message comes through loud and clear: the difficulties of making are still with us, and they dictate the course of contemporary art much more than most artists and curators would like to admit. Successful facture is something like a tide line in contemporary art, which helps us see whether individual practices are sinking or swimming.

And this brings me, finally, to Isabelle Cornaro. While many artists are furiously treading water, trying to keep afloat in the currents, she swims at ease within the ocean of production. Cornaro takes for granted the absolute importance of the physical making of her works (photographing, scanning, molding, displaying), always chosen on purpose because for her these processes—whether she is doing the work herself or delegating it—are significant in themselves. She embraces it as primary content, just as the index was for Krauss. Indeed, Cornaro serves as an excellent case study for comparing the present moment with that of 1977, because she so routinely employs indexical means in her work. Paramount among these is the technique of life-casting, a craft with deep historical roots, extending back through the didactic plaster casts made across Europe and America in the 19th century to the astonishing grotesques of the 16th-century French potter Bernard Palissy. These precursors point to a truth that perhaps eluded Krauss, situated as she was in the late stages of conceptualism: an index, even if direct, can be extremely difficult to make. Palissy's chargers, festooned with every manner of lizard, frog, shell, and fern, exhibit awesome technical mastery. They also are replete with associations grounded in process (for Palissy himself, life casting was infused with divine overtones because of its similarity to the fossil-making that God conducted through the geological actions of the earth).[4]

4 On this point see Michael McKeon, *The Secret History of Domesticity: Public, Private and the Division of Knowledge*, Johns Hopkins University Press, Baltimore 2005.

It is ironic that Palissy's intensely naturalistic works should be so inspirational for Cornaro, for as she says, her own interest lies primarily in the "denaturalization" of given aesthetic categories. "What we call a 'minimal' black line on a piece of paper," she writes, "may arise from a totally metaphoric and 'figurative' process; or a cast heap of kitsch objects may be the result of a purely nominalist gesture and thus be quite 'abstract.'"[5] Instead of medium specificity, Cornaro explores media mutability, alchemical transformations that cross the apparent gaps between one discrete process and another. She encourages us to read a museum exhibition display, or a seemingly random disposition of gold jewelry, as a landscape painting. Architectural moldings are pressed

5 Isabelle Cornaro, personal communication with the author, June 24, 2010.

together into freestanding sculptures, without losing their vocabulary of supplementarity. And in two related series entitled *Moulages sur le vif (Vide-poches)* (*Life Casts [Catch All]*, 2009–2011) and *Homonymes* (*Homonyms*, 2010), indexical processes are brought face to face with the found objects that they reproduce. In the former series she employs a large scanner, as opposed to a conventional camera, to embed three-dimensional objects into a two-dimensional array. The *Homonymes* are realized with the collaboration of a specialist fabricator (as Cornaro does not disdain such recourse to others' skills), and like the arrangements of found objects that they copy, present an array of decorative and useful items on tabletops, as if a still life painting were laid out on a dissecting table. All these "flatbed" compositions (to appropriate Leo Steinberg's term,[6] originally applied to Robert Rauschenberg, but perhaps even more appropriate here given Cornaro's use of a scanner) are nominally contained within this genre of still life. Yet they also read, again, as landscapes, or perhaps urban design models. This is the dizzying flux that Krauss dreaded—a play with mediums that might almost be whimsical. Yet Cornaro knows that no matter how rootless and subjective her works become, materiality and process will hold them in a cogent framework. The absolute difference in affect between original and cast, for example, provide a stable ground in an otherwise vertiginous viewing experience.

6 Leo Steinberg, "The Flatbed Picture Plane," from *Other Criteria: Confrontations with Twentieth Century Art*, University if Chicago Press, Chicago 2007, first published 1972.

Making, then—no matter who is doing the making—serves as Cornaro's anchor. It gives her what Krauss wanted for art: an objective center, on which to build a meaningful practice. And yet she has achieved this through something nearly opposite to Krauss' vision. In place of iron-clad presence, her indexicality is a sort of gamesmanship. Instead of the constancy of medium, she skips like a stone from one medium to another, subjecting each in turn to her scenographic vision. Photography, casting, video, drawing: all are part of this endeavor, and each has their specificity. In Cornaro's hands—at work in the young 21st century, not the dying embers of the 20th—the particularity of production is nothing more (or less) than the passport to the new.

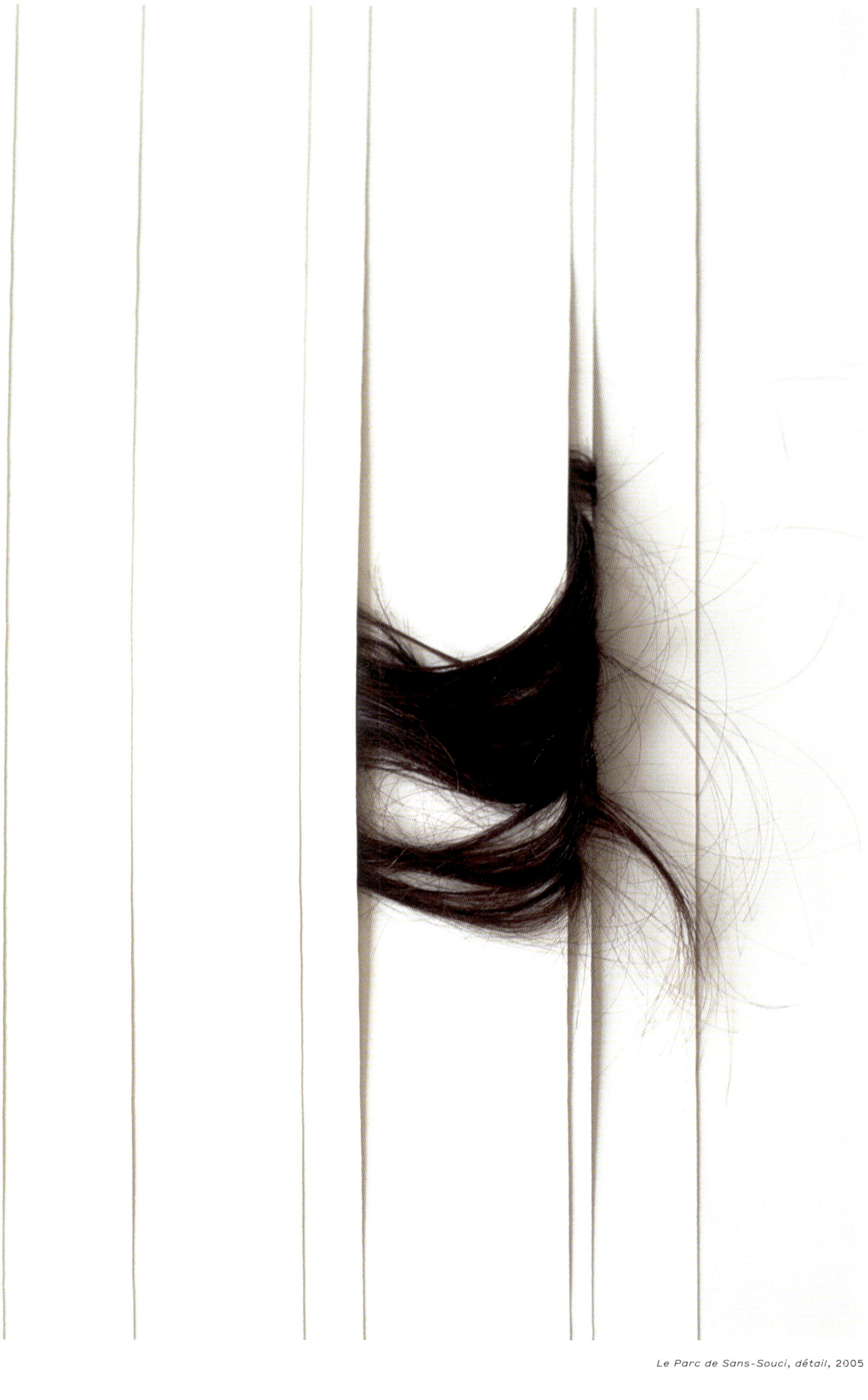

Le Parc de Sans-Souci, détail, 2005

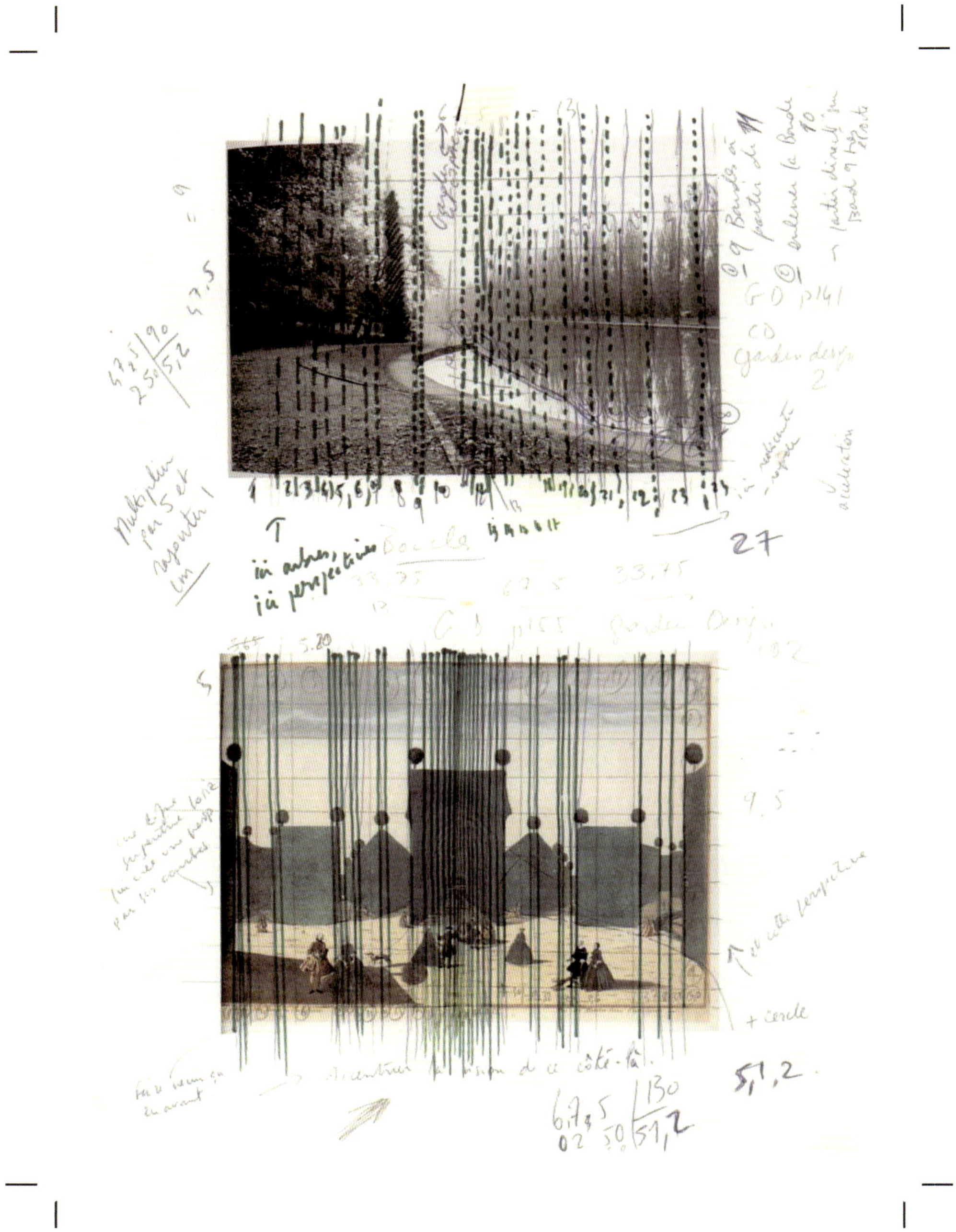

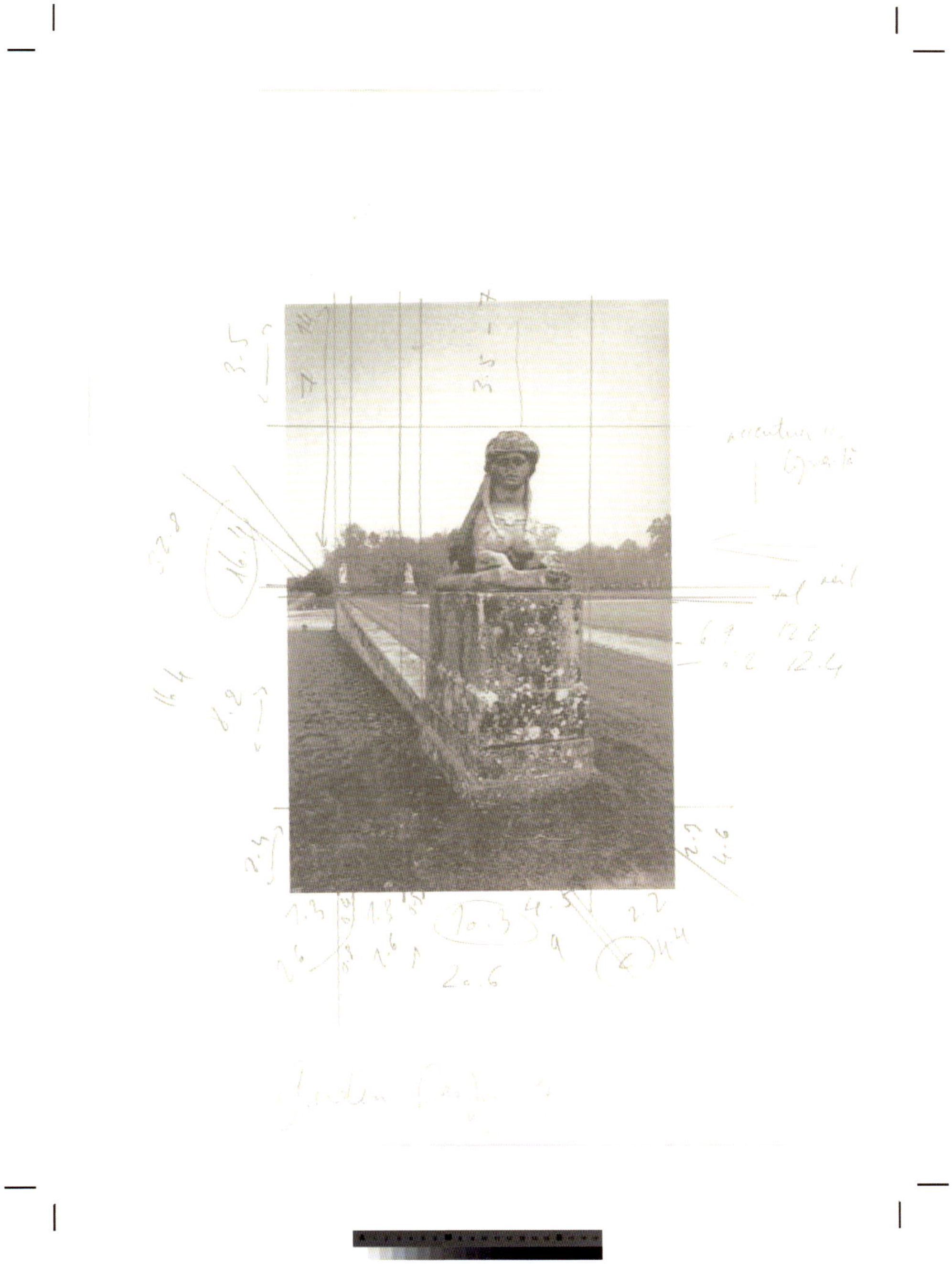

Bons à tirer, 2008

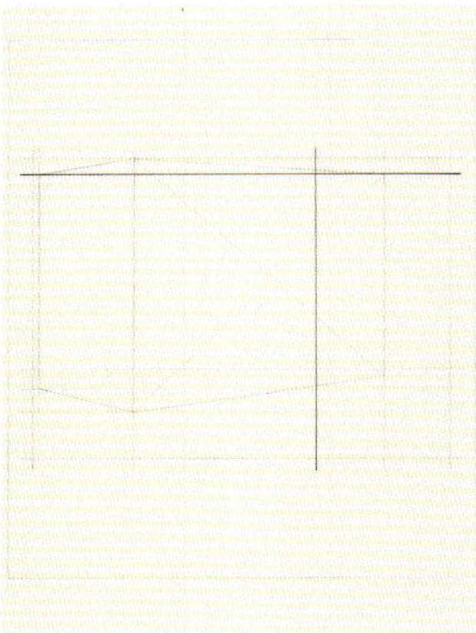
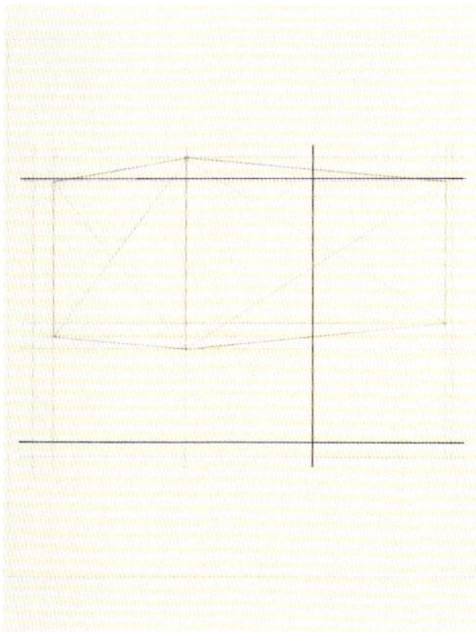
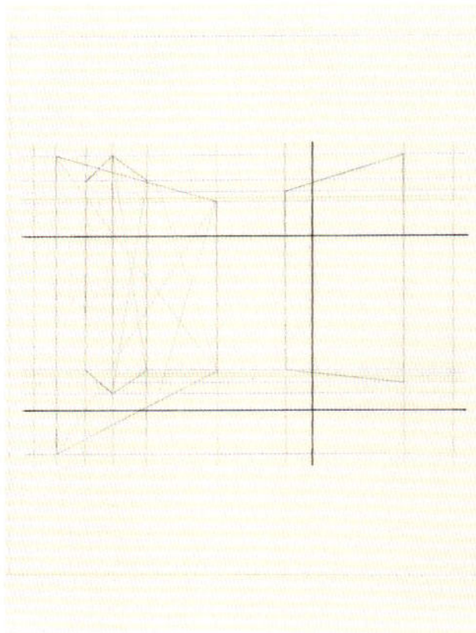
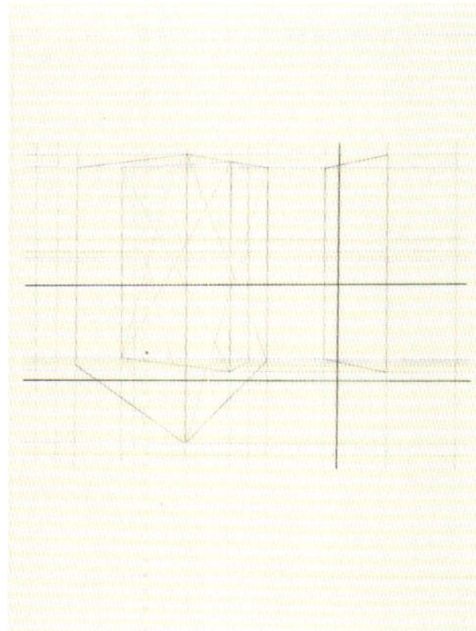
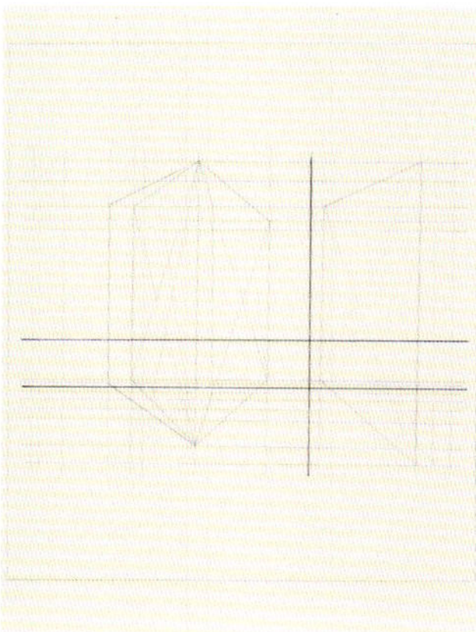
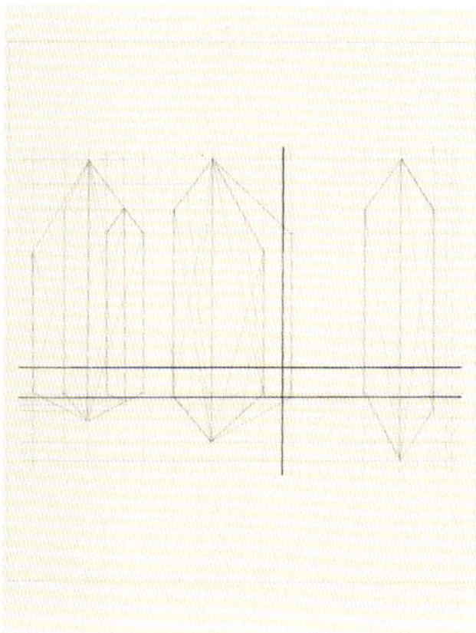
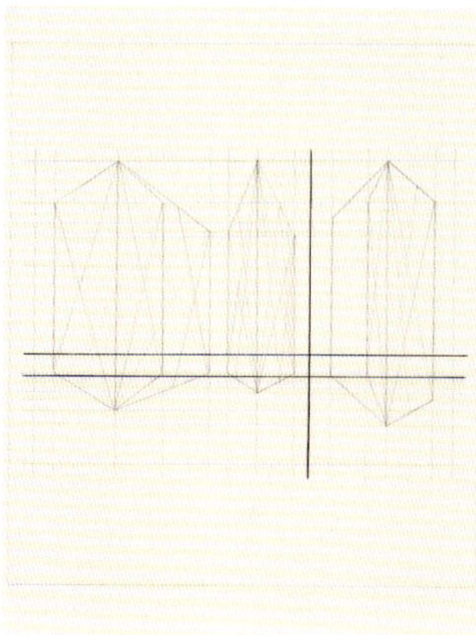

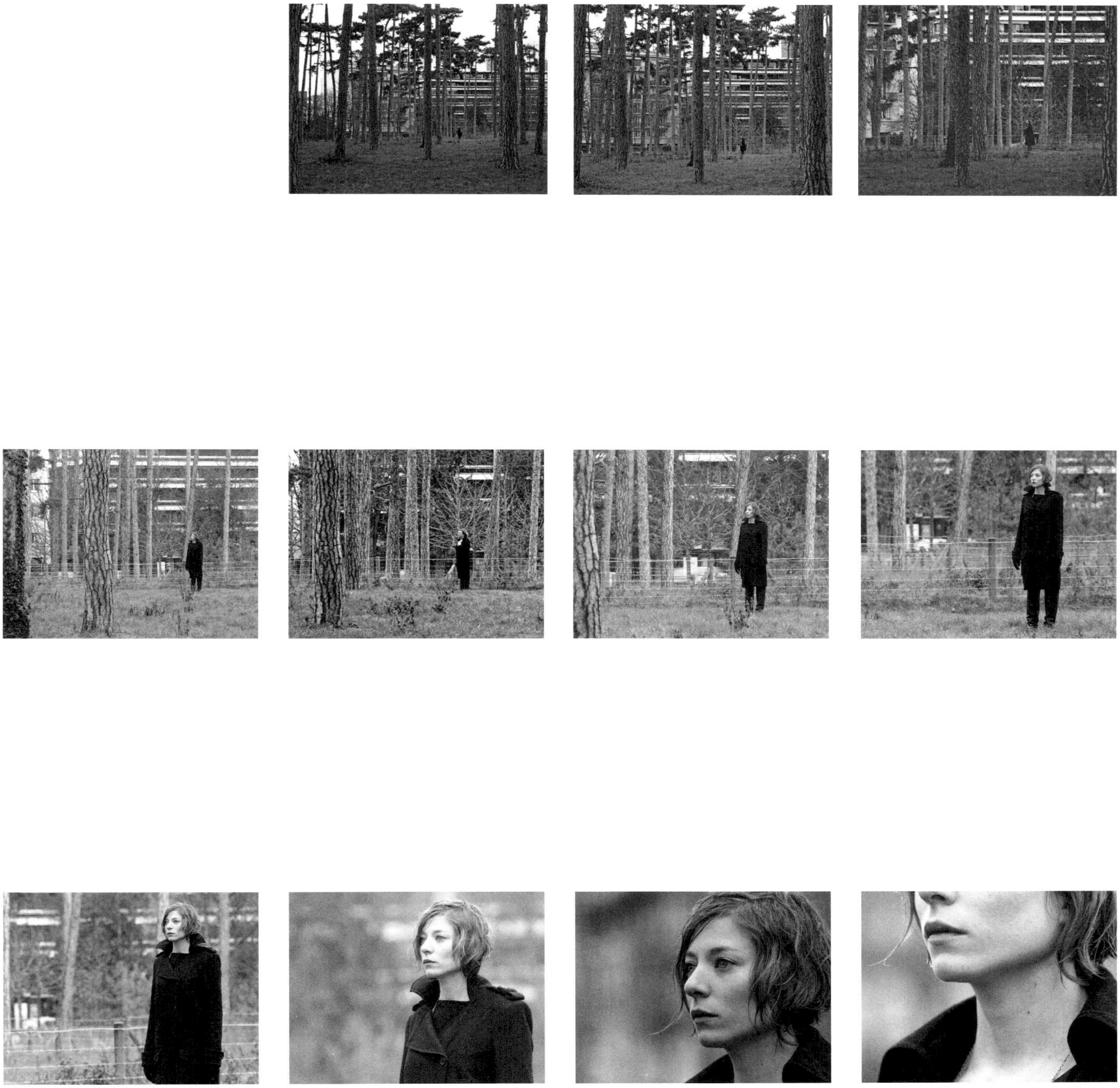

Black Maria (Phenomena Overwhelming Consciousness), 2008

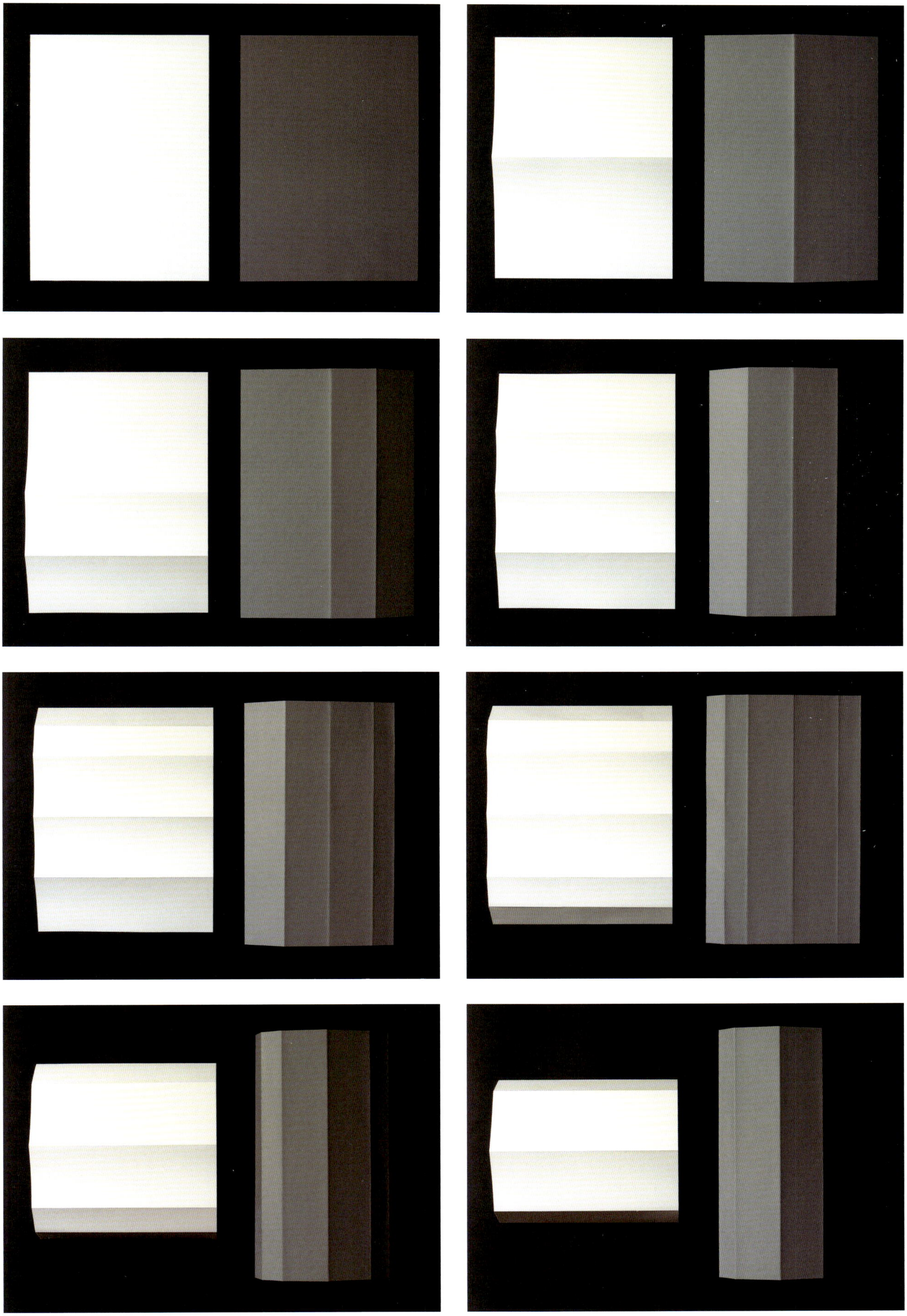

Cinésculptures (Polyèdres), 2008

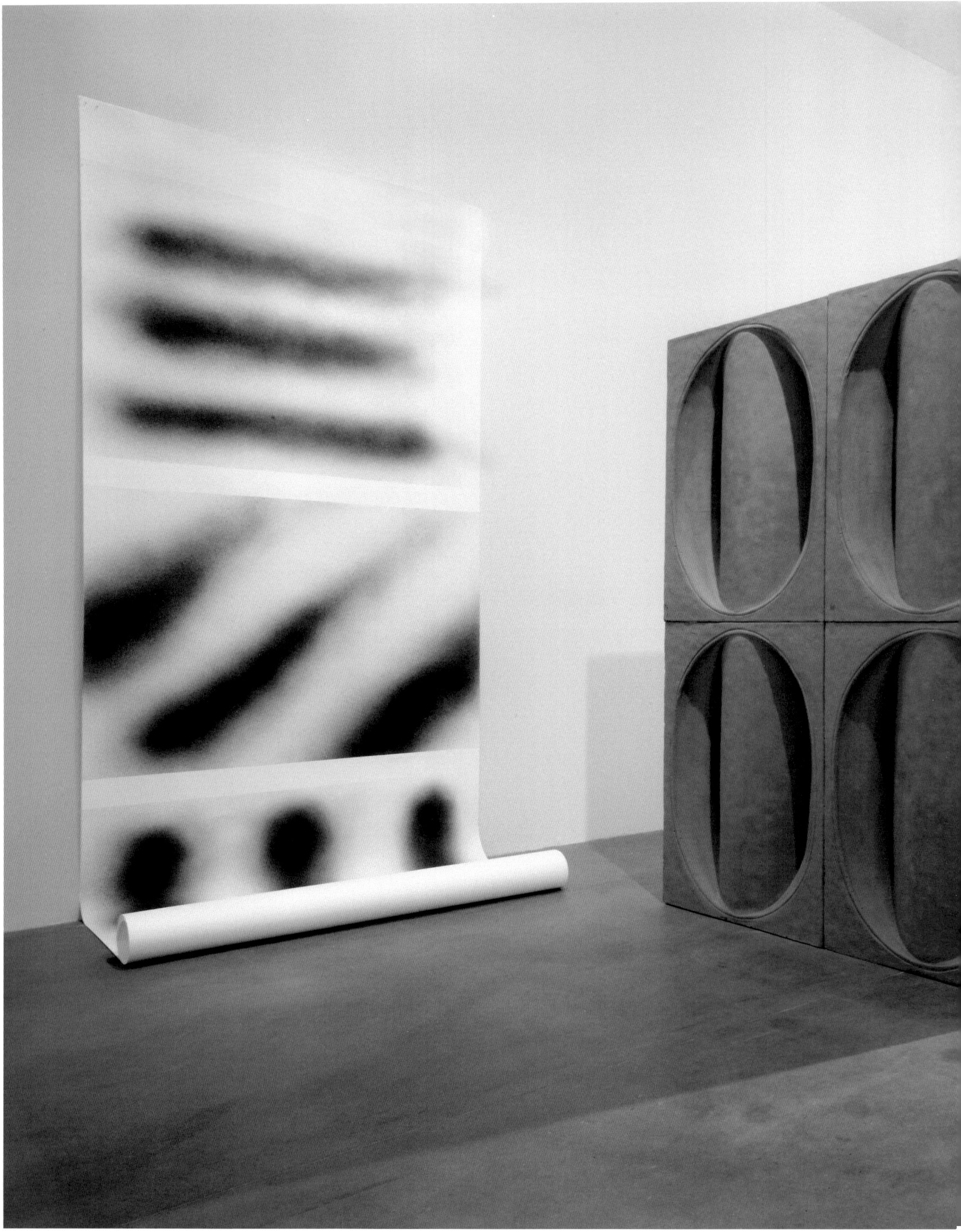

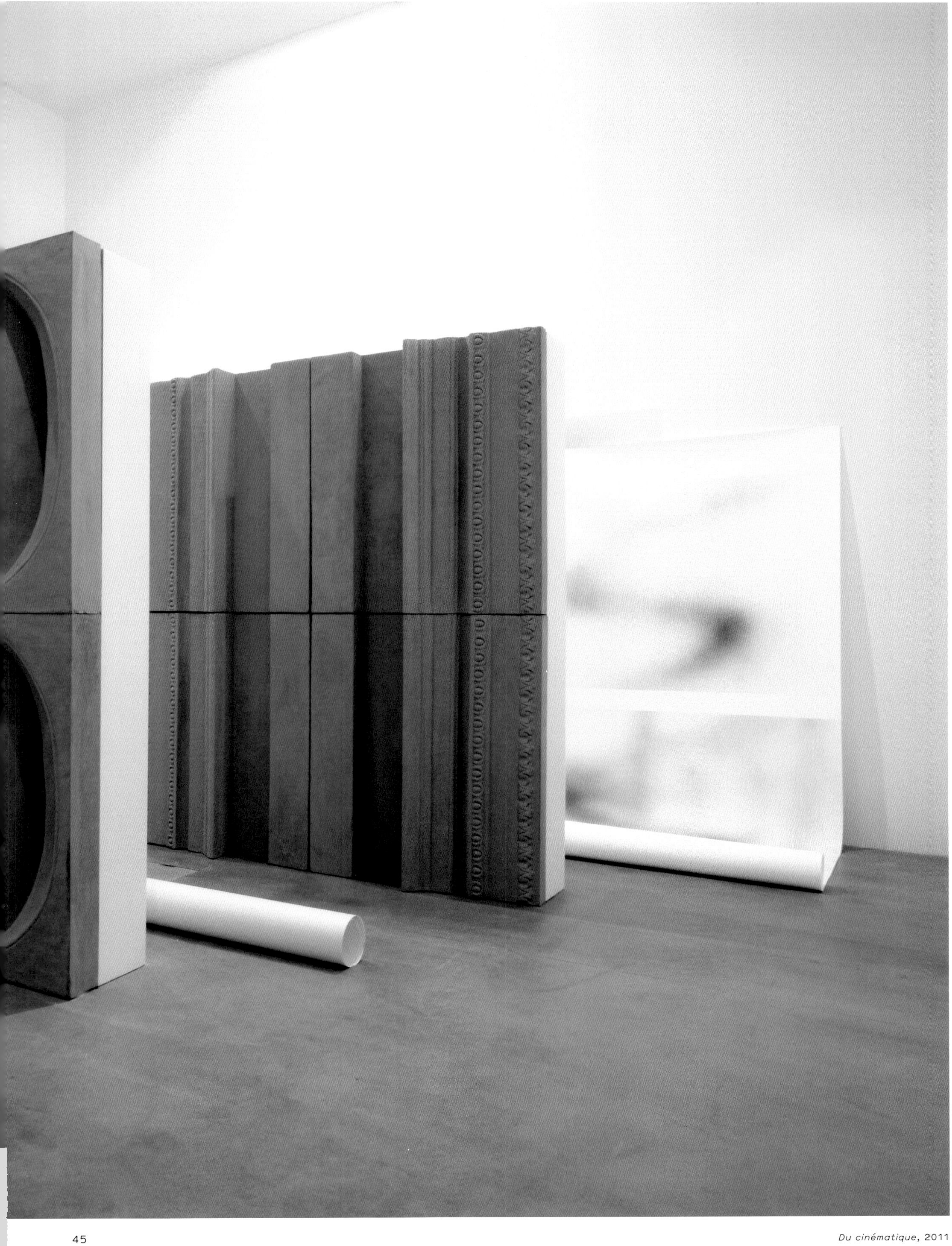

Du cinématique, 2011

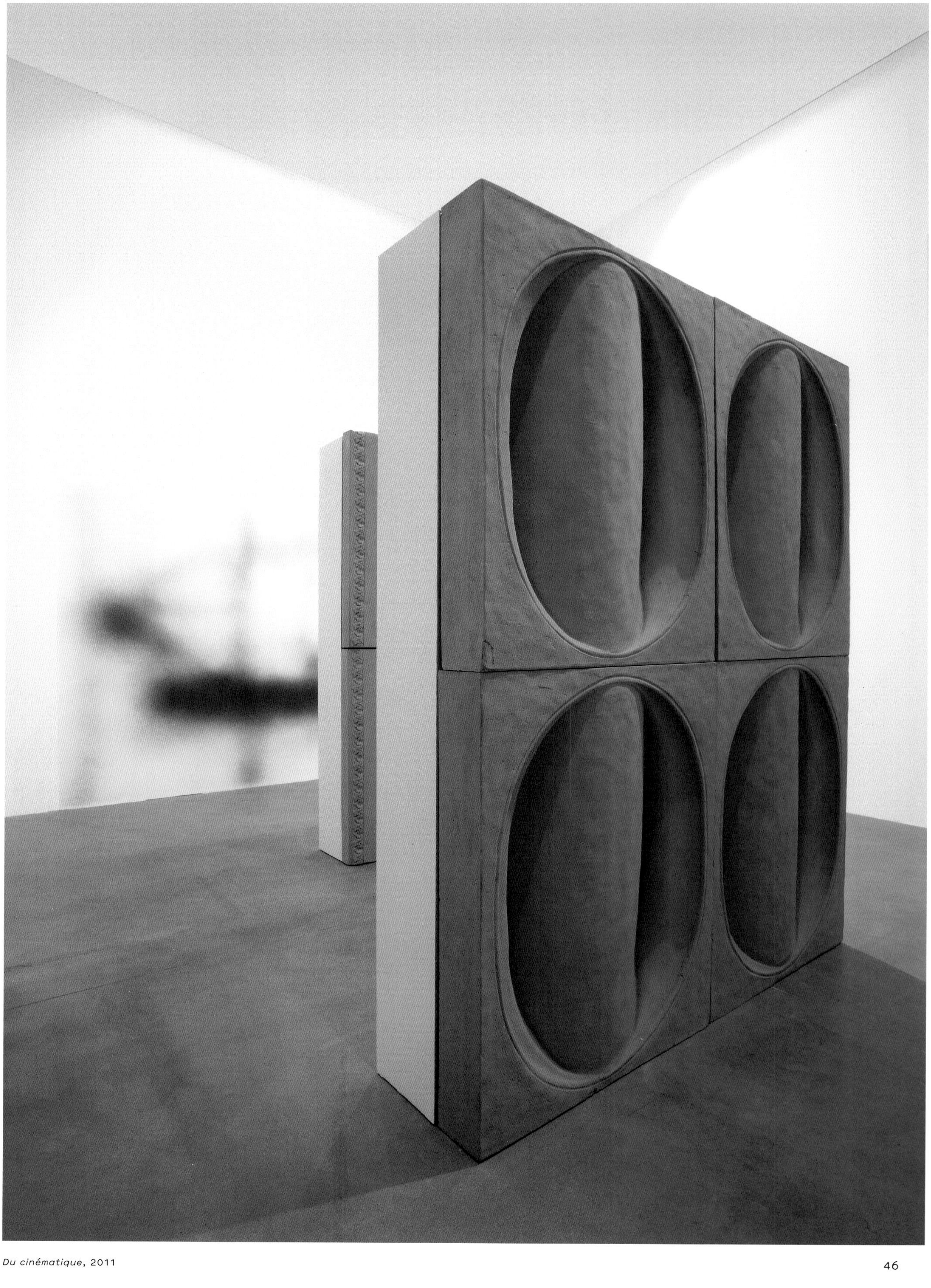

Du cinématique, 2011

From the Cinematic to Display
Interview with Alice Motard

ALICE MOTARD In May 2011 you presented an installation at a show called *Un'Espressione Geografica,* held at the Fondazione Sandretto Re Rebaudengo.[1] Your installation, *Du cinématique* (*On the cinematic*), was composed of casts of architectural features and spray paintings. This piece embodied a synthesis of the conceptual and formal concerns operating within your work. It was the first time you were led to react so directly to a context—a geopolitical context, at that. How did you respond to the invitation to go to Apulia, and how did you use the experience to produce new works? In short, how did you proceed in the context of this "commission"?

1 *Un'Espressione Geografica: Unità e Identità dell'Italia attraverso l'Arte Contemporanea* (May 2011–January 2012) was organized by Francesco Bonami and Stefano Collicelli Cagol to coincide with celebrations of the 150th anniversary of the unification of Italy. The exhibition was based on voyages made by 20 artists from various European countries, each of whom traveled to one of Italy's 20 regions.

ISABELLE CORNARO I decided to reflect upon certain aspects of the region's dominant baroque aesthetic—namely, the importance of staging, the highly constructed perspective, and the propensity of static elements to evoke movement—all the while seeking to maintain a certain degree of abstraction with respect to the context. So whereas the casts of architectural fragments refer directly to the facade of the basilica of Santa Croce in Lecce,[2] the spray paintings were based on images from an already existing film, *Floues et colorées* (*Blurry and Colored*, 2010).

2 The basilica of Santa Croce was the work of the city of Lecce's finest architects. Its construction lasted from 1549 to 1695 and represents the most accomplished example of the particular version of baroque architecture developed in the Lecce area in the 17th century, marked by teeming, exuberant sculptural decoration both inside and out.

ALICE MOTARD The monumental and authoritarian impression made by the installation is quickly mitigated by the beholder who, in order to take in the full measure of the piece, has to wander among the various elements and become immersed in the experience. A kind of back-and-forth circuit then arises between the abstract marks on the paintings and the mimetic, stylized ornamentation of the sculptures, which the beholder experiences and tries to make sense of. It's ultimately the beholder who creates the "montage."

ISABELLE CORNARO These different types of marks struck me as simultaneously mimetic and abstract, even though each maintains a different relation to the object of reference, which is more recognizable in the casts than in the paintings. They were staged in the same way as the elements of the works *Paysage avec poussin* (*Landscape with Chick*), proposing a non-linear reading similar to cinematic montage. The spray paintings, based on a film about the various stages of the composition of a painting, also entailed a film-like temporal sequence, here deployed in space. The identical casts of architectural features, however, are more closely related to photography—the molds were handled like carefully composed shots, cropped from a larger ensemble, and are potentially reproducible on a mass scale.

ALICE MOTARD There is also the optical effect of the disappearance and reappearance of paintings and sculpted panels as the beholder adopts different viewpoints on the work. This game of hide-and-seek reminds me of Richard Serra's in-situ work for the Grand Palais in Paris in 2008.[3]

3 Richard Serra, *Promenade,* 2008, steel, five elements each 1700 × 400 × 13 cm (approx. 56 × 13 × ½ ft), produced for the *Monumenta 2008* exhibition at the Grand Palais in Paris.

Does the use of this type of illusionistic procedure also relate to baroque art?

ISABELLE CORNARO The spatial arrangement of the individual elements mimics an idealized perspective, because the gaps between them diminish as a function of their physical distance across the room. In this respect, the work alludes to the construction of viewpoints, which has baroque connotations, as does the immersive aspect of the whole installation. I tried to dissociate the volumes from the surfaces by placing the casts in the center and relegating the paintings to the surrounding walls. The texture of the paintings—that "powdery" mixture of black and white—plus their lack of color and the fact that they slide to the floor, makes them seem like layers of dust, evoking the worn stone at Lecce.

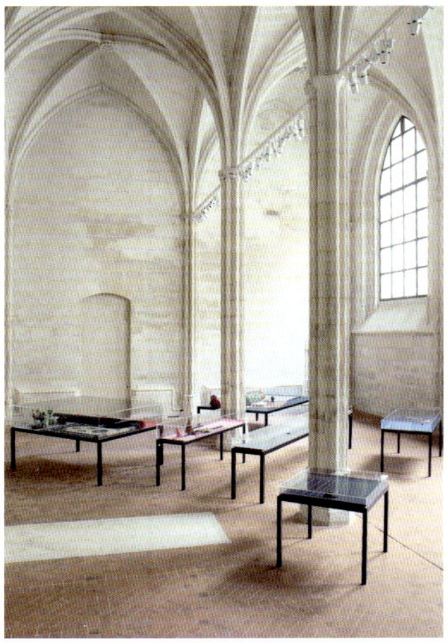

Le Proche et le lointain, 2011
Exhibition view, Collège des Bernardins, Paris, 2011

ALICE MOTARD If we look at it literally, doesn't this work represent your attempt to remedy the phenomenon of erosion that you've just mentioned and, more metaphorically, your struggle to stave off a certain depletion of forms and imagery? It seems to me that what you're creating with this somewhat funereal installation is like a freeze-frame, to stick with the movie analogy.

ISABELLE CORNARO The hieratic nature of the casts, combined with the paintings that decompose a cinematic sequence, certainly have something of the quality of a freeze-frame—or maybe a clumsy memorial—about them. The decomposition is not just a way to multiply the images, but also functions like slow-motion and close-up shots of the original sequence.

ALICE MOTARD Notions of reproduction or reproducibility—whether artisanal (hand-crafted) or industrial (mechanical)—are central to your work, where the distinction between original and copy is constantly called into question. The *Homonymes* (*Homonyms*), for example, are copies—done by hand, but using the mechanical process of casting—taken from originals that don't survive the process of reproduction. So the copies paradoxically become unique—their silicon molds have to be destroyed in order to remove each of the four casts, preventing multiple copies. Meanwhile, the series *Moulage sur le vif (Vide-poches)* (*Life Casts [Catch All]*) is the product of "cuts" made in the matrices of life-size scans of random compositions of objects. Each print represents a new "cut" from the matrix, hence is *de facto* unique. Were you trying to invalidate the notion of the original the better to invalidate the notion of reality?

ISABELLE CORNARO I never really thought about it in those terms. The ambiguity of the status of the "original," treated mainly as a referent, results from a process of successive transformations—copying, re-using—that is a constituent part of my work. The question of the status not only of objects but also of the context in which they are perceived interests me, but the nature of the specific status—original work or copy—ultimately matters little. Instead, I wonder where the "original act" resides. For the series *Moulage sur le vif* the composition was done through framing, not through the placing of the objects, which I either arranged without thinking or delegated to someone else. The absence

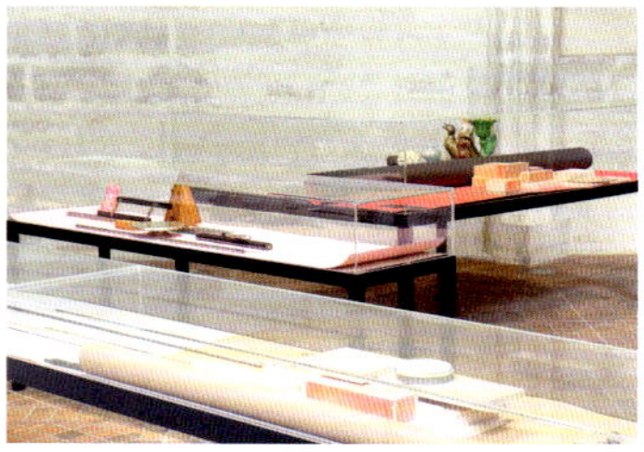

Le Proche et le lointain, 2011

of subjective involvement at the moment of placement was reinforced by the mechanical reproduction of the "scanner," because these are casts of "images."

ALICE MOTARD The analogy with a film editor, who works from images shot by someone else, is telling here. Your production process is characterized by a balance between what I'd called "letting go" (a rejection of subjectivity that is apparent when you allow a system, or chance, or someone else to take over) and "terrific control" over the final act (whether it deals with choice of medium, choice of framing, or display—or, usually, all of them together). At the Collège des Bernardins you placed an entire series of readymade objects—taken from Western commercial culture—on colorful surfaces in display cases set in the former sacristy. How did you conceive the spatial organization and arrangement of the objects? These objects, which you describe as "emotionally charged" or "symbolically meaningful," can be seen in many of your works, so anyone familiar with your oeuvre will recognize them. Does "putting them under glass" in a hallowed setting constitute a halt to the constant circulation you had previously imparted to them?

ISABELLE CORNARO The installation functions on the tension between an initial perception of the work from a distance—an overall vision—and a complementary or contradictory view of the objects close up. The idea of the overall design of the display cases was to produce a geometric shape that occupied the space in a dynamic way, which explains the diagonal angles and the use of large colored surfaces. The arrangement of objects was based on balanced relationships of mass (full versus empty) and varied visual approaches (organized and controlled versus heaped and piled), borrowed from existing works.

ALICE MOTARD So was the collective impact of the objects—their group dynamic—more important than their use value, exchange value, or symbolic value?

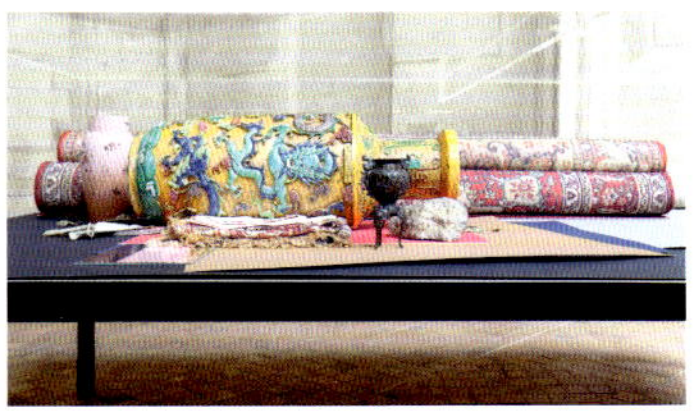

Le Proche et le lointain, 2011

ISABELLE CORNARO The objects were arranged according to categories (decorative motifs, naturalist figures, etc.) that were then violated through shifts from one area or display case to another. I wanted to test the impact of these objects from the standpoint of their direct use, so they were less distanced than the ones in *Paysage avec poussin* and *Moulage sur le vif*. The "glass cases" were a technical requirement—they contributed an additional connotation that I had to incorporate, but the work could have existed without them.

ALICE MOTARD In contrast, *Du cinématique* is completely free of these fetishes of civilization. Should the two installations be seen in tandem?

ISABELLE CORNARO In a way. Even though the elements in *Du cinématique* are much more abstract and linked more to architecture than to everyday objects and furnishings, the use of heterogeneous cultural components (from the baroque, the history of painterly abstraction, photography) and the "montage" operation that the beholder has to perform are pretty similar.

ALICE MOTARD The elements which make up *Du cinématique*—which one can basically describe as paintings of films and sculptures of architecture—result in a transfer of themes from one medium to another.[4]

4 Cornaro's operating method was described as "re-mediation" by Marjolaine Lévy in "Isabelle Cornaro—cet obscur objet du désir," *Artpress* 377 (April 2011).

ISABELLE CORNARO These transpositions make me think of the term "homonym," meaning words with the same visual appearance but different meanings. The decision to use the same motifs across different media, and consequently to dissociate the motif from its mode of representation, underscores the autonomy—that is so say, the intrinsic significance—of the medium. This decision also raises issues of resemblance and referent, which might be an object or an idea, or both at once. For example, the sculptures called *Homonymes* function on two levels of resemblance: to objects (casts of everyday objects) and also to artistic categories (naturalism, stylization, abstraction). I think the structural re-casting of a form or literary style, as analyzed by Alain Robbe-Grillet in *Pour un nouveau roman* (*For a New Novel*, 1963), is linked to a quest for realism. Experimenting with different modes of representation means constantly asking the same question: how can you approach the polysemy and polymorphy of things?

ALICE MOTARD I understand that one of the bas-reliefs of the facade of the Basilica Santa Croce in Lecce that you have reproduced and serialized, is a stylized representation of the voluminous sleeves which were fashionable in Renaissance Italy. Can representation be endlessly self-referential without going around in circles?[5]

5 I have borrowed the phrase *retournement de la représentation sur elle-même* (representation revolving upon itself) from an article by Marie Canet, written for Cornaro's exhibitions of films at the Galiere Cortex Athletico in Bordeaux, July–September 2010. Available on-line at http://chinese-girl-film.blogspot.com/search/label/Isabelle%20Cornaro (accessed September 1, 2011).

ISABELLE CORNARO I don't think so. Neither in my own work, nor in general. I use certain models and certain items (notably "tautological" objects) because they are codified and loaded with an additional symbolic or emotional meaning. The pitfall would be to empty them of meaning, to completely neutralize images. I prefer to see it as the continuous introduction of additional formal, poetic, and discursive propositions. It's the idea of "and": being one thing *and* another thing *and* yet another thing. One of the issues in this whole process that intrigues me involves hierarchy, that is to say processes of demoting and re-promoting under a different system, which I think are essential to the creation of works of art.

ALICE MOTARD Was the fact that Gerhard Richter began to use painting as a "photographic medium" in the 1960s, thereby reinvigorating painting, of any significance to you when you were envisaging your own artistic path?

ISABELLE CORNARO I haven't particularly thought about it, but I've always appreciated Richter's multiplicity of forms, which can be antagonistic without being contradictory. And the way in which each composition is simultaneously a form (including everything about form that is irreducible to language) and a problematized reflection on that form. Which also applies to Bruce Nauman and his way of getting a distance on individuality and a certain expressiveness of the body through the use of written texts, and to Marcel Broodthaers' use of transpositions (painting, film, text) to analyze the structures of the field in which he worked.

ALICE MOTARD These artists developed a reflection on nature and the role of the artistic act and, more broadly, on the relationship of the individual

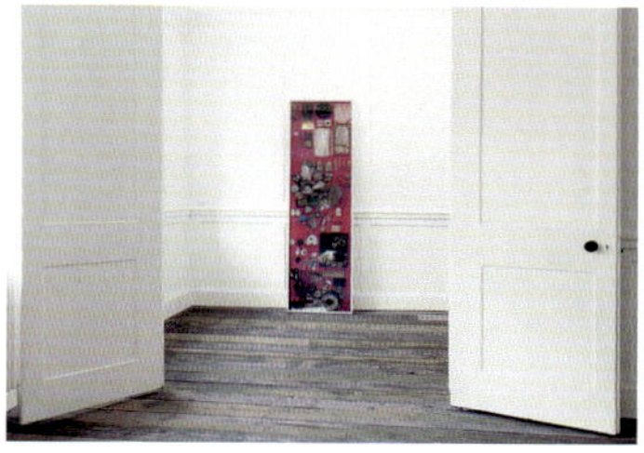

View of the exhibition *Unto This Last*, Raven Row, London, 2010
Moulage sur le vif (Vide-poches), 2009

to society through a constant questioning of the structures that govern social, political, artistic, or architectural recognition—which goes far beyond what some people call "institutional critique." Is the way they staged things, in a kind of theatricalization, also something that interested you?

ISABELLE CORNARO That's right, in so far as these contrived systems create contexts for experimentation—physical, emotional, intellectual—that don't deliver up their codes (apart from a few keys to decipherment). And thus they don't impose a codified use or meaning.

ALICE MOTARD Do you already know what your future works will look like?

ISABELLE CORNARO Just now I'm thinking about incorporating elements that have a certain "pathos," combined with witty or absurd things that would create a distance from that pathos. For the moment it's all highly speculative. They're just ideas in the air, yet it's almost always the collision of several apparently unrelated ideas, along with a few half-formed images, that wind up outlining something new.

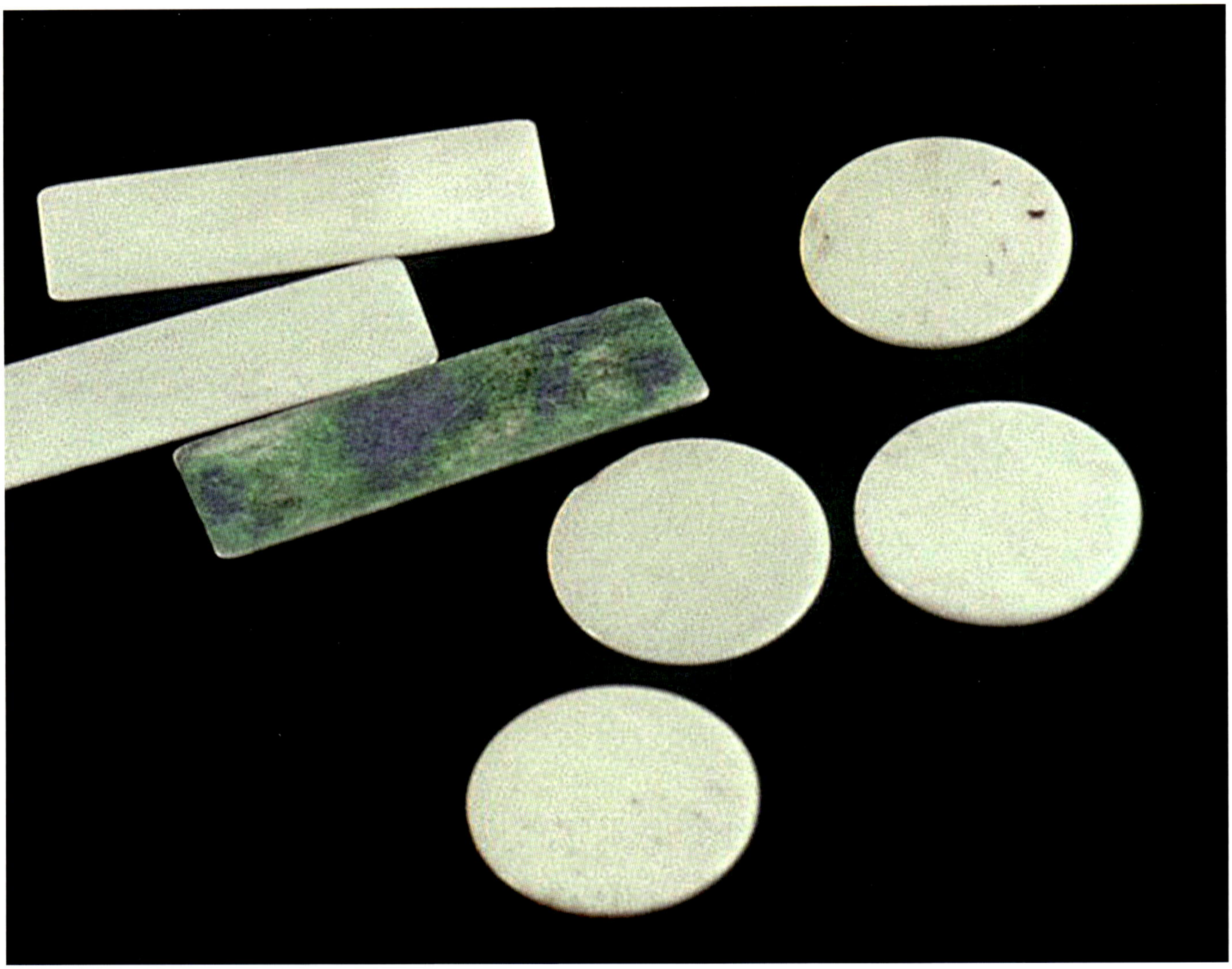

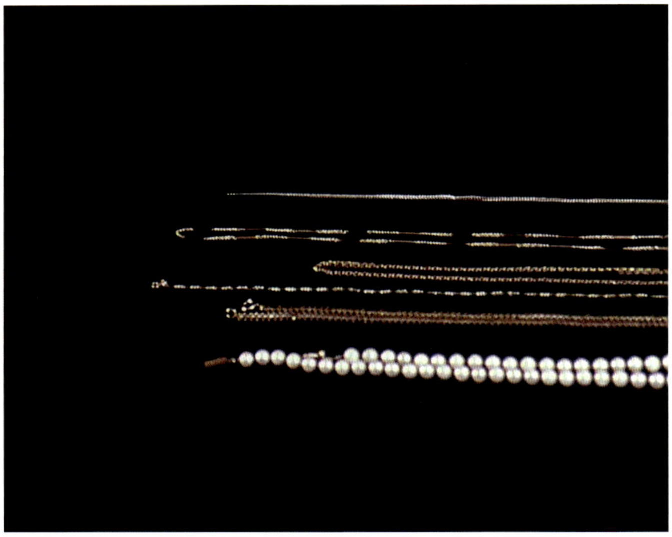

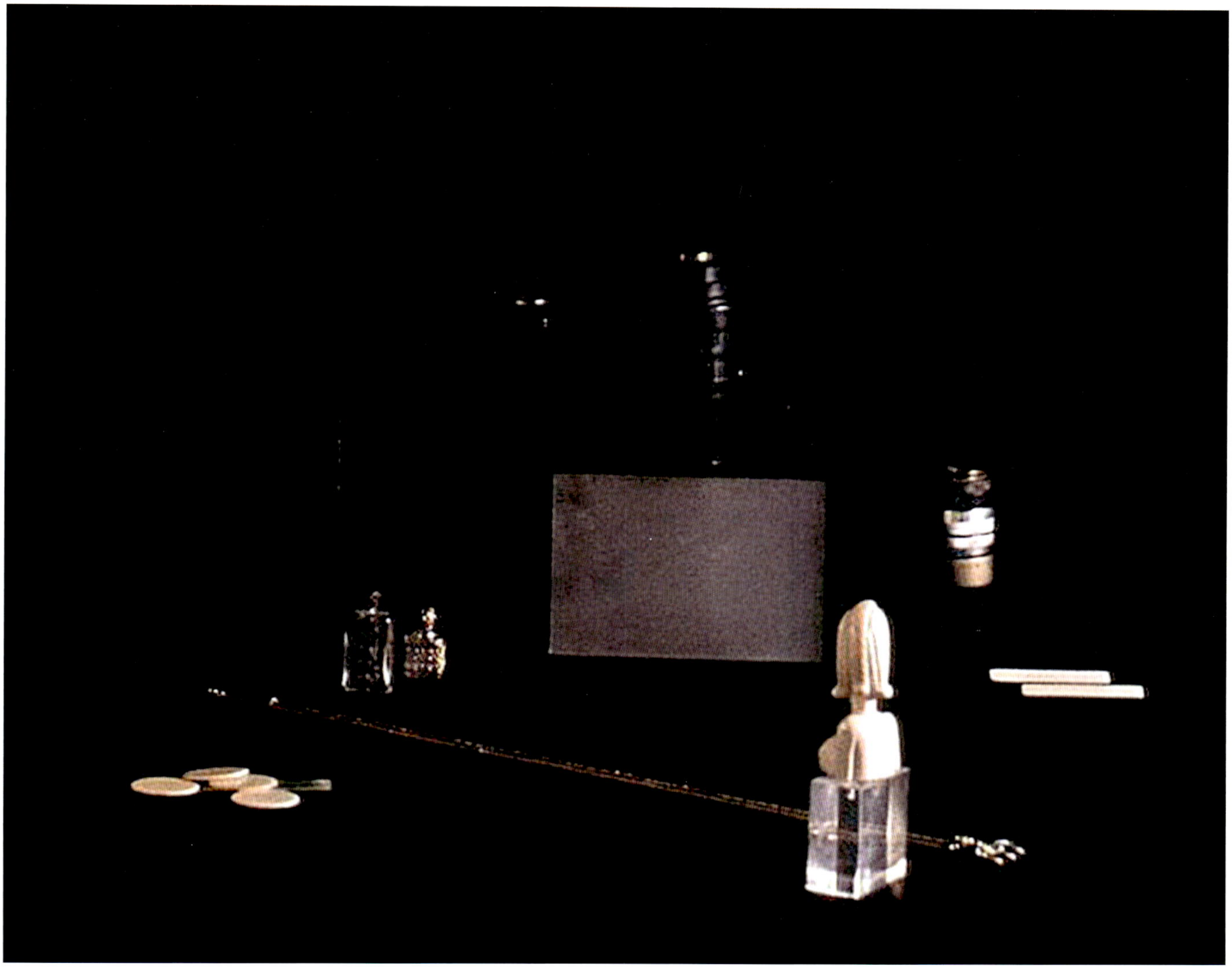

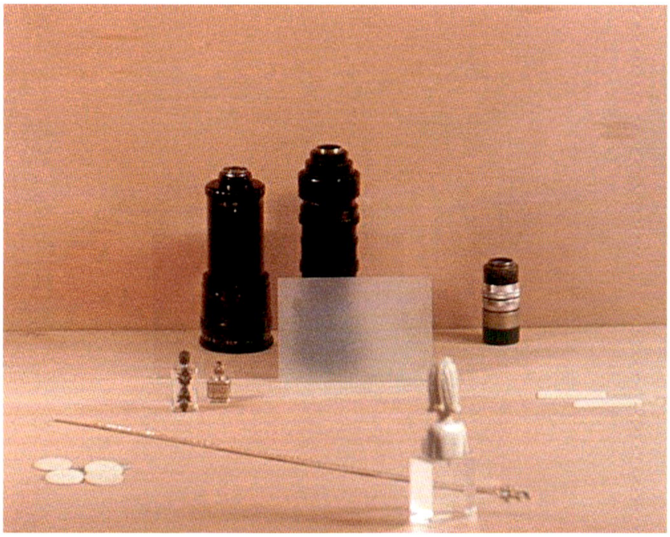

Premier rêve d'Oskar Fischinger, 2008

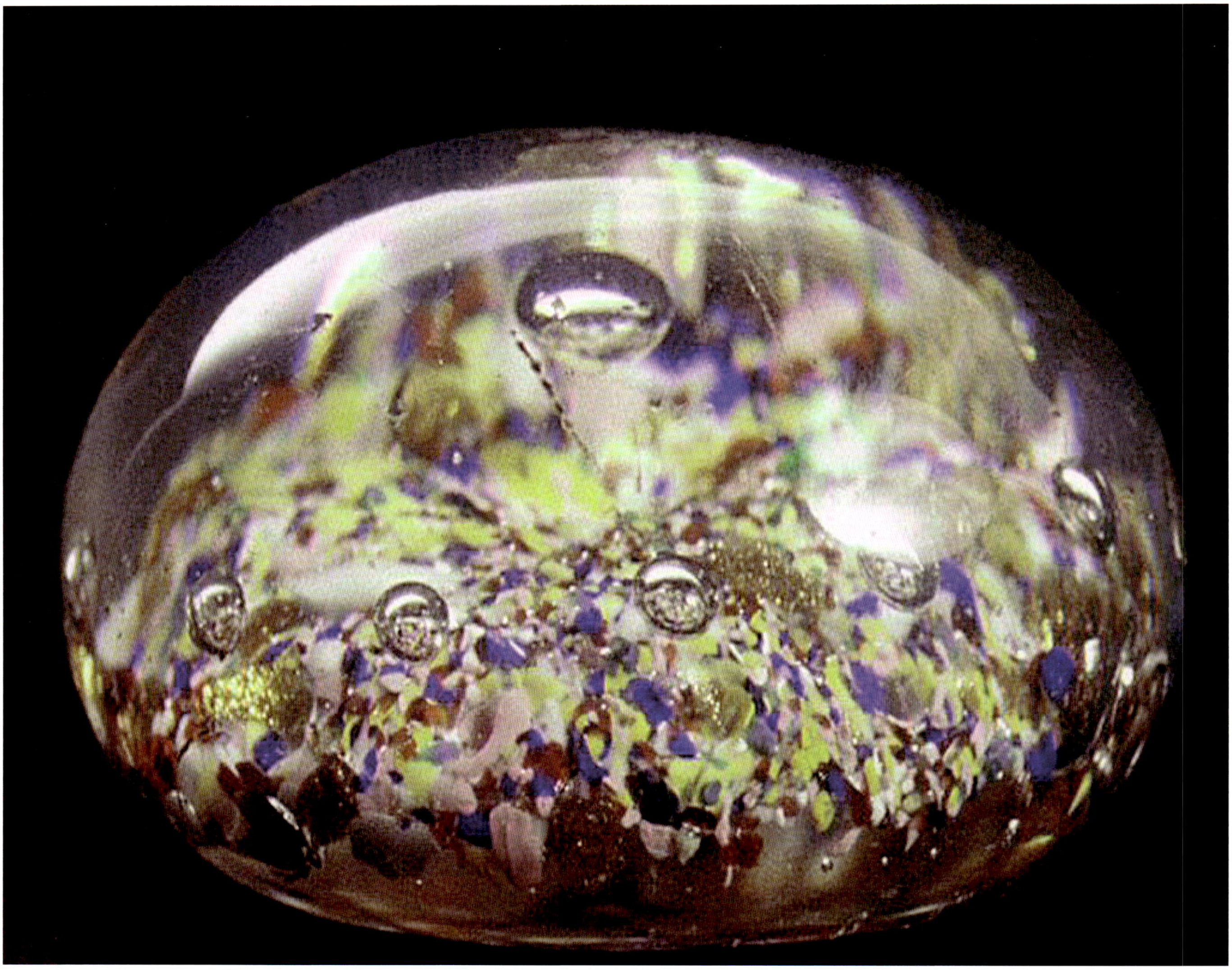

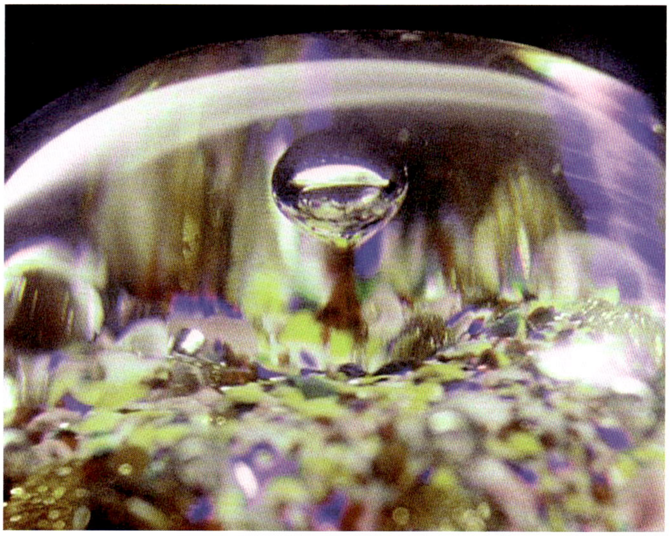

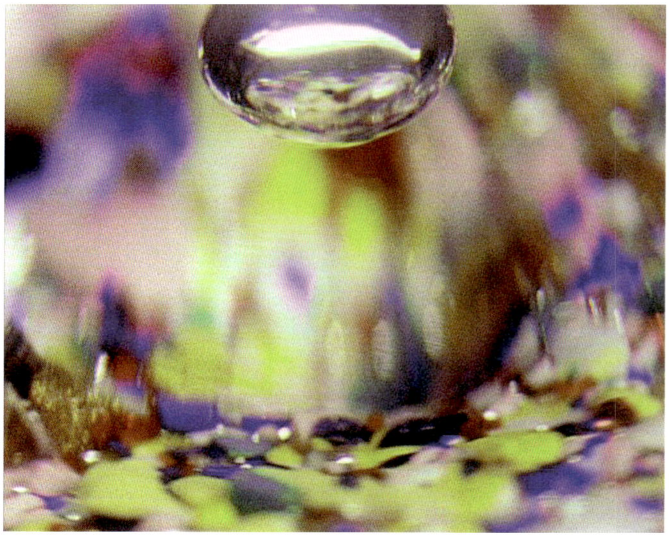

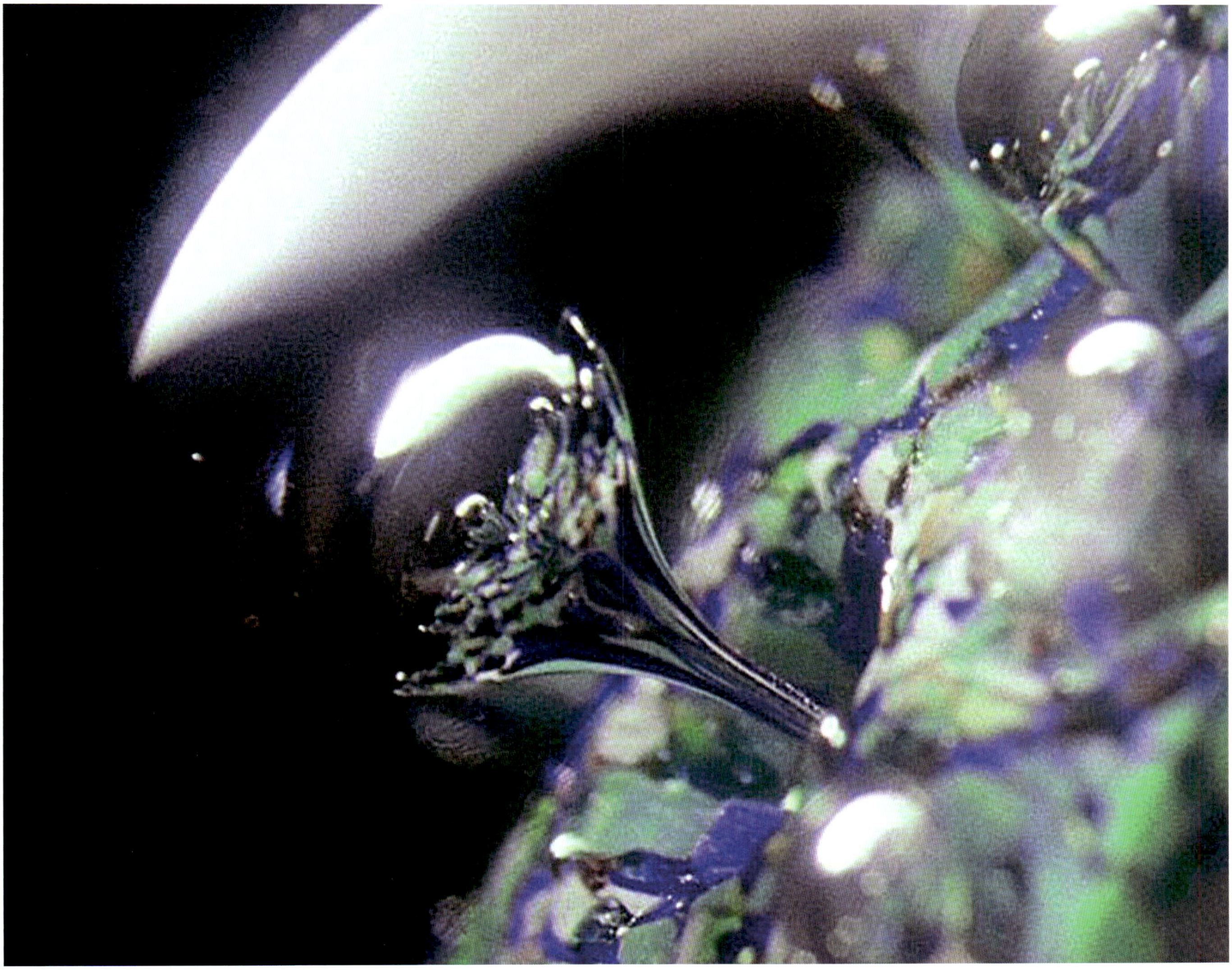

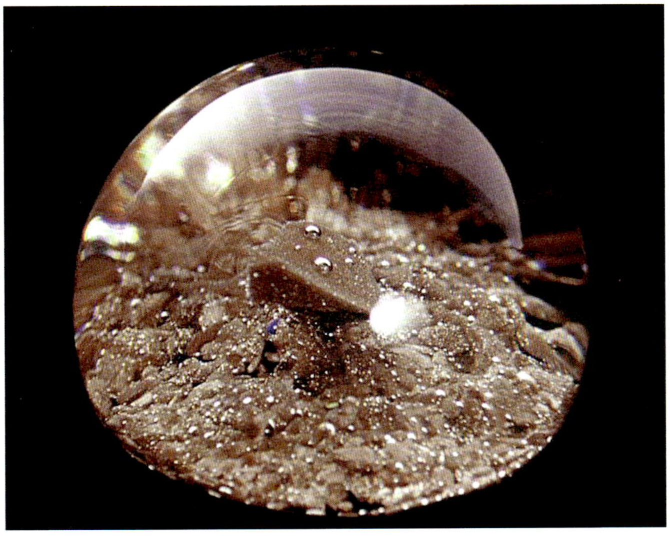

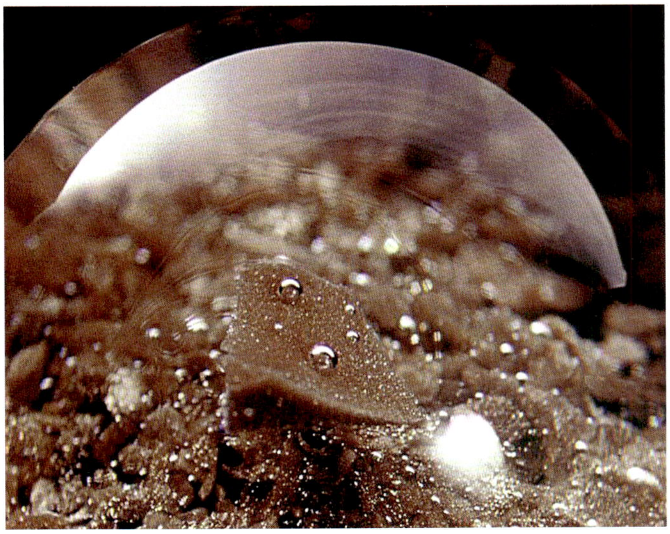

Premier rêve d'Oskar Fischinger, 2008

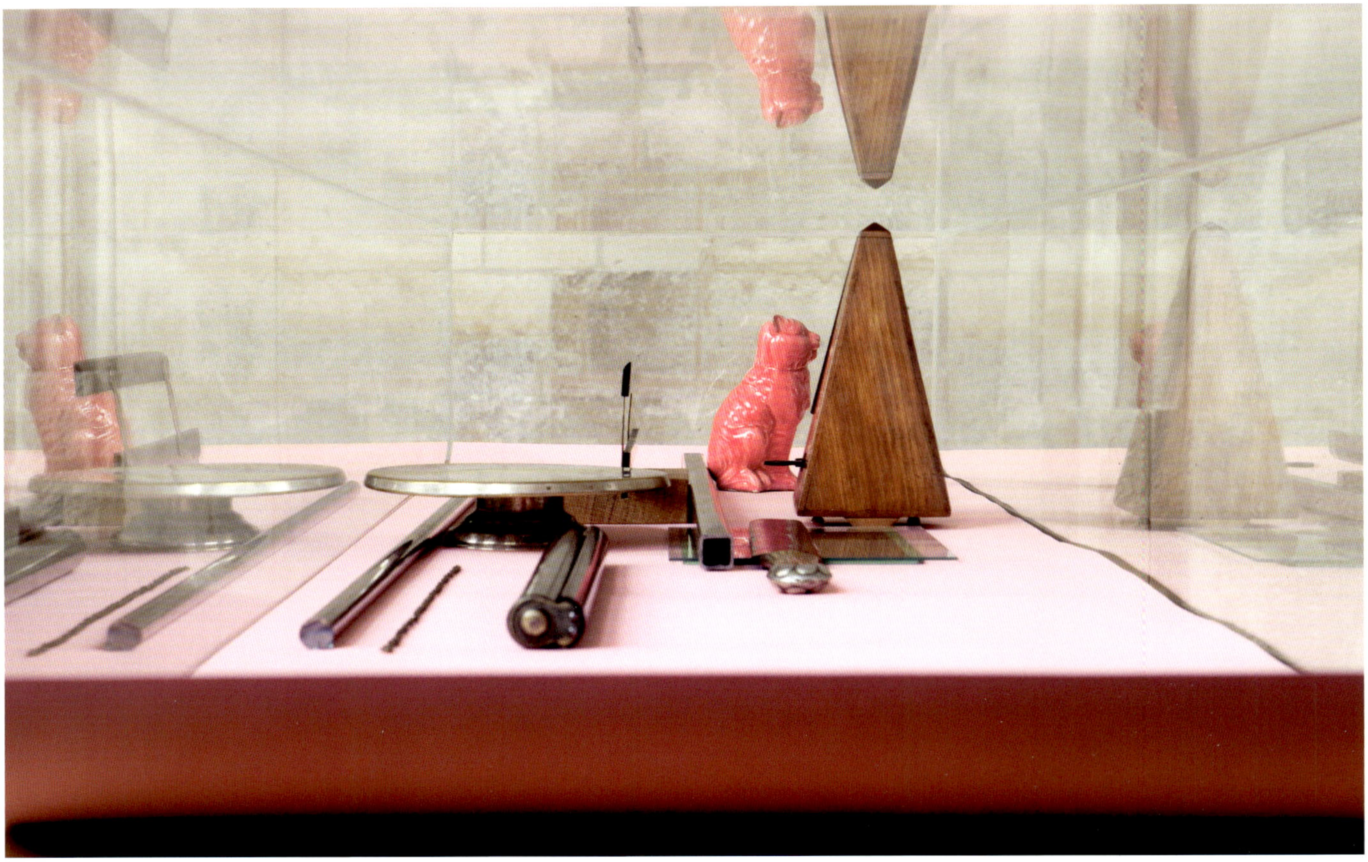

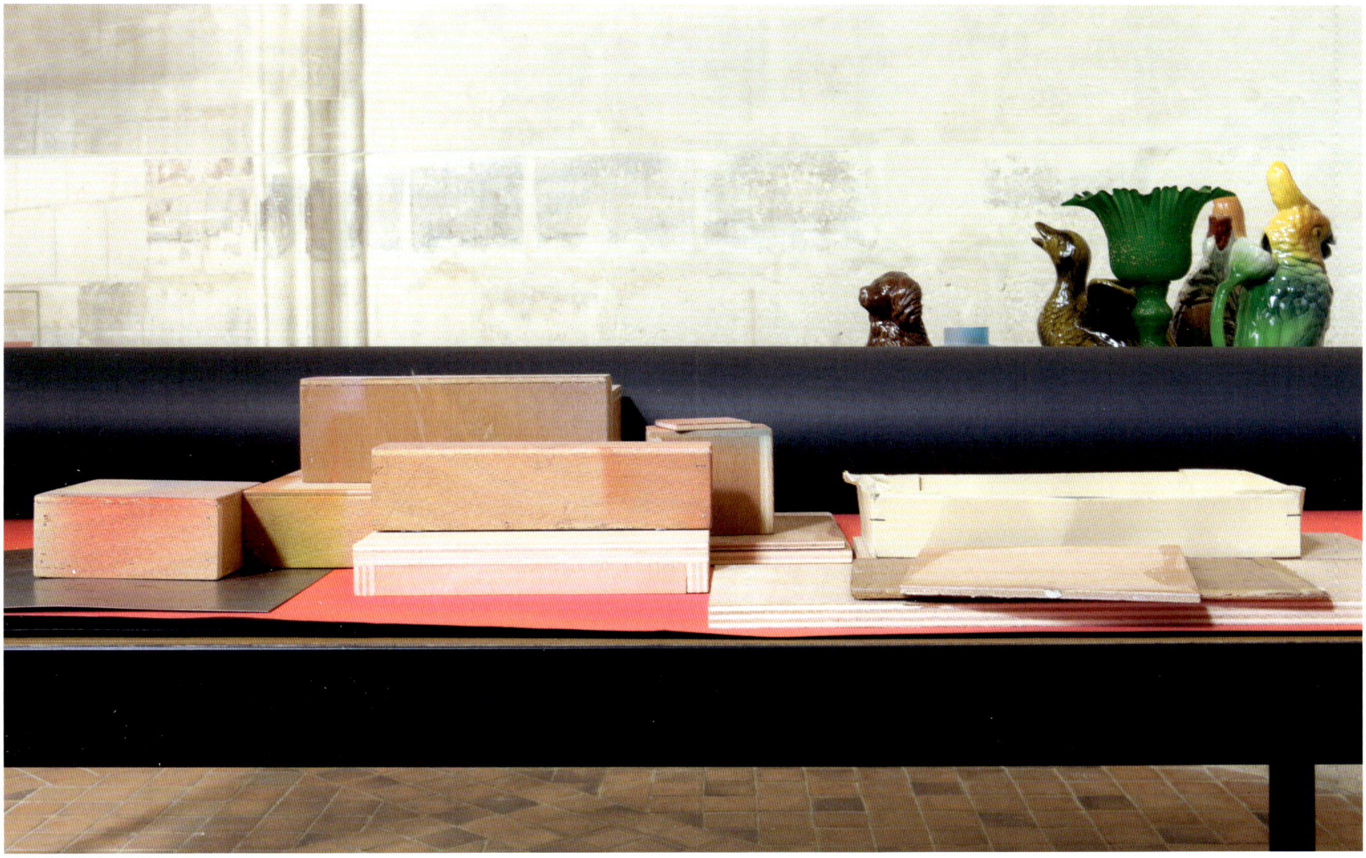

Le Proche et le lointain, 2011 (details)

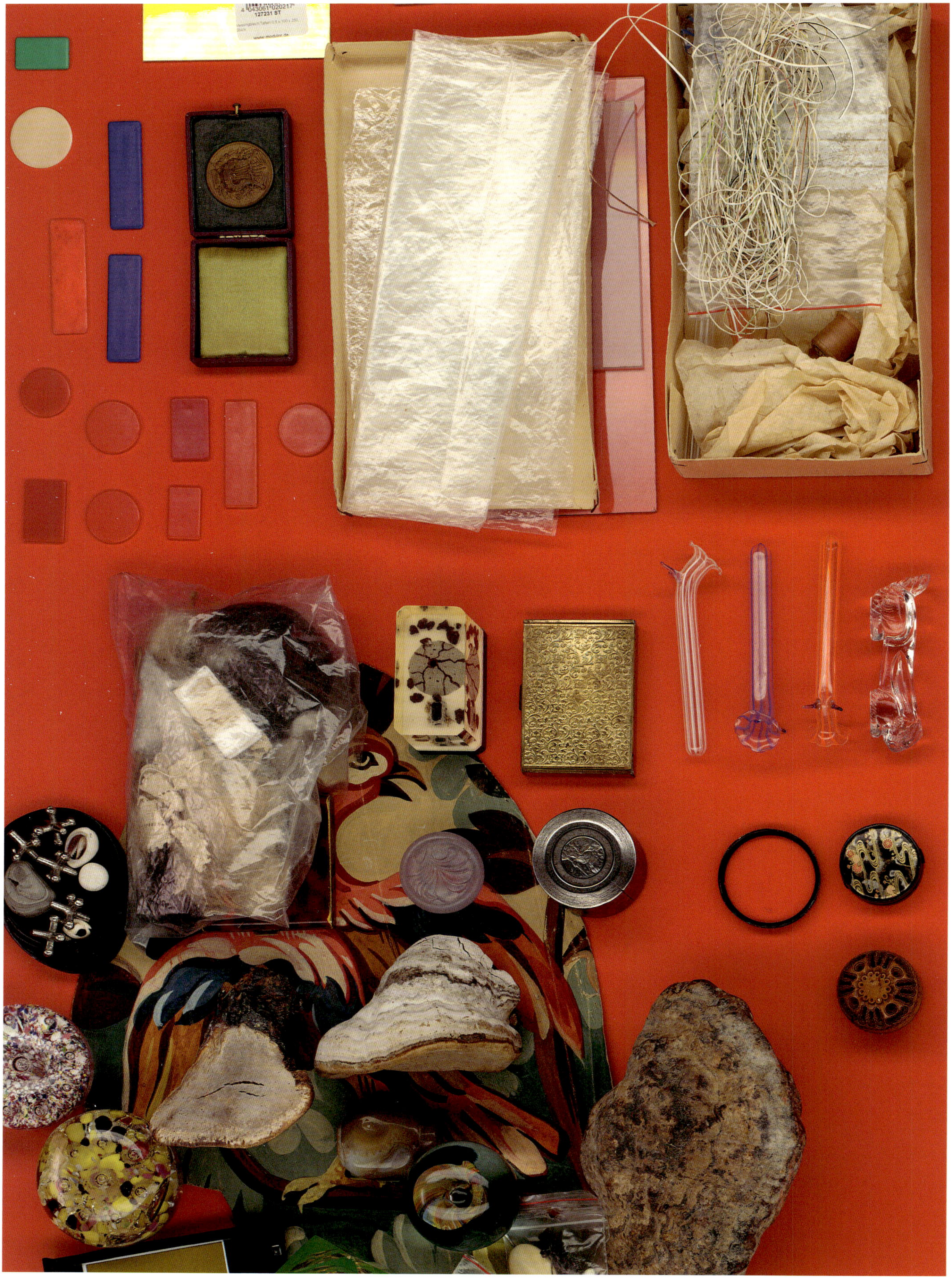

Moulage sur le vif (Vide-poches), 2011

Artist in the Act
Clément Dirié

In 2001, Isabelle Cornaro recorded her laughter and displayed her arms in a video piece titled *Vanité à vif* (*Quick Vanitas*). It was a rare instance of the artist's own body being present in her work. We see her handle the symbolic, codified objects that make up a still life. In a paradoxical gesture, she brings life to an inanimate genre of painting, cutting it to the quick by decomposing and analyzing its construction. Meanwhile, in her spray paintings called *Impressions* (2010), Cornaro traveled in the opposition direction, deconstructing a video work to produce a series of still images; for *Cinésculptures* (2008), she studied the effect of folding and shadows on black and white paper; and for *Moulage sur le vif (Vide-poches)* (*Life Casts [Catch All]*, 2009–2011), she dissected an overall image into as many details as were required to "empty" it. In *Vanité à vif*, it was the artist who herself "emptied" the depiction—as her arm composed it, her laughter superimposed a critique of the moral philosophy that stems from the canonical vanitas genre of still-life painting.

Although the "act" is as primordial for Cornaro as the "making," it is rarely underscored—as it is here—through the presence of her body. Only the *Songs of Opposite* (2008) also feature the artist's body, although in these video pieces she becomes just a figure, a line in space, a tool for measuring a typically French landscape.[1] In *Vanité à vif* and *Songs of Opposite*, the artist gets into the *act*. In her other works, all that remains is the trace of her intervention: just an indication of her action, a mere incarnation of the artist. Her works stem from acts of installing, collecting, casting, photographing, scanning, filming, framing, decomposing, tracing, and so on. These acts decompose depiction, revealing the ways in which the human organization—indeed, domination—of reality (through classical pastoral landscape, formal gardens, figures on coinage, etc.) is manufactured. Such acts efface the human figure—in particular that of the artist—to the benefit of human beholders and various other kingdoms (vegetable, mineral, minimal, inert) that function as "eyewitnesses."

1 The body was similarly simplified to a line in Cornaro's series *Parc de Sans-Souci*, in which locks of hair—like inert objects elsewhere—represent elements deployed in space.

The series titled *Bons à tirer* (*Blueprints*, 2008) is characteristic of Cornaro's approach, underscoring the creative process. Cross-sections and a color chart stress the process of manufacture, while lines and annotations reflect the artist's thought processes in selecting, framing, and calculating the arrangement of objects, landscapes, and artworks. *Bons à tirer,* which is both a study for *Le Parc de Sans-Souci* (*The Grounds of Sans-Souci*, 2005) and a sketch that has acquired the status of an autonomous artwork, demonstrates that what interests Cornaro is not so much representation as the *process* of representation, not making so much as *mechanisms* for making, not the value of things so much as the value *adopted* by the things to be represented. In this respect, landscapes, jewels, decorative objects, and the vocabulary of

Minimal art—indeed, Cornaro's sources draw on idioms from wide-ranging historical periods—are tools designed to produce shifts from one regime to another, to explore processes of equivalence and translation, and to quicken—through her very *acts*—the modalities of artistic representation and reproduction.

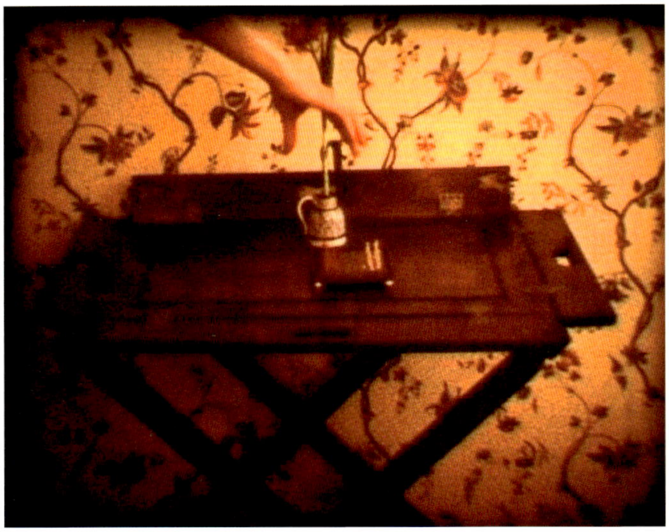

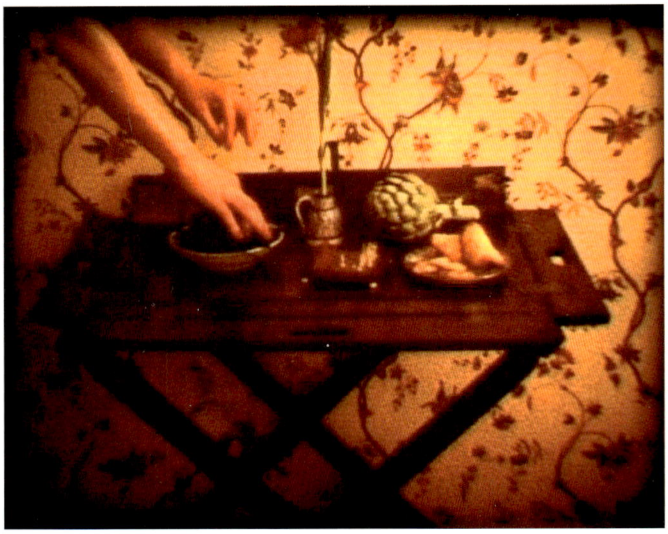

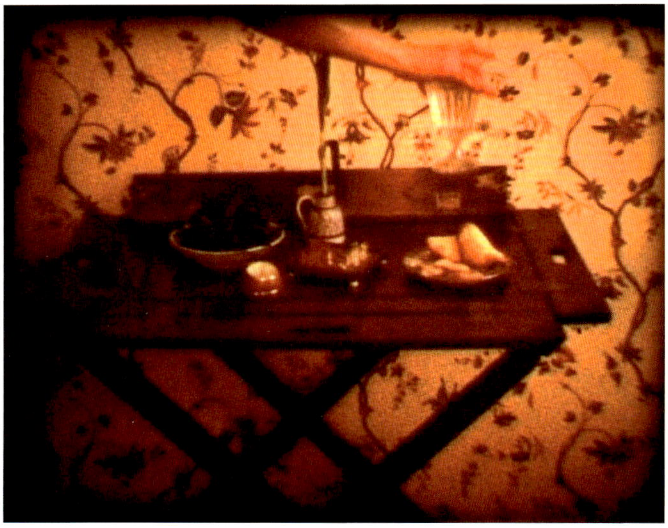

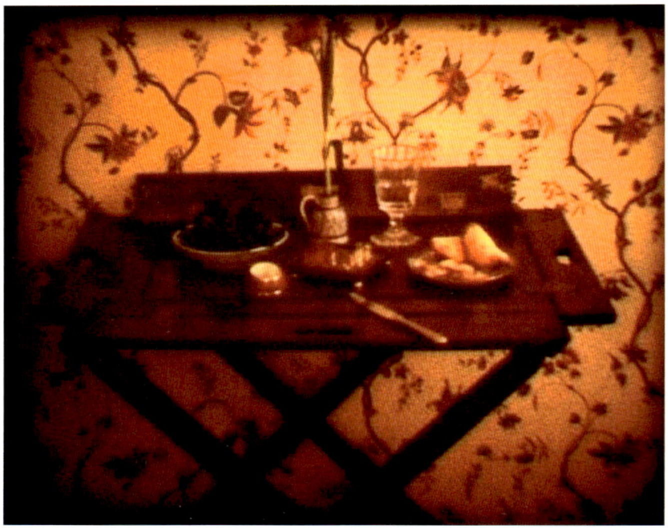

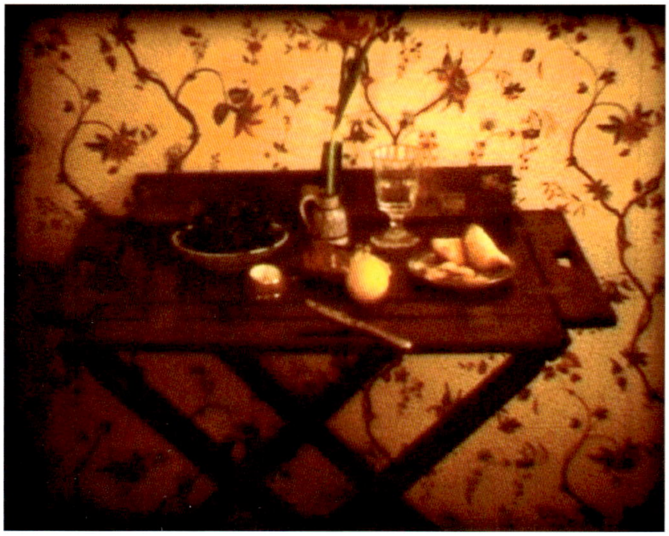

Vanité à vif, 2001

List of Works

p. 2–3, 4
Paysage avec poussin et témoins oculaires (Version III), 2010
Installation view and details
Plywood plinths and panels, various objects, circa 400 x 500 cm, maximum height: 300 cm
Exhibition view, Kunsthaus Glarus, Glarus, 2011
Photo: David Aebi, Burgdorf
Collection Musée national d'Art moderne, Centre Pompidou, Paris

p. 6
Paysage avec poussin et témoins oculaires (Version II), 2009
Plywood plinths and panels, various objects, circa 400 x 500 x 280 cm
Exhibition view, Museum of Modern Art, Warsaw
Courtesy Piktogram/BLA, Warsaw, Poland

p. 8
Landscape with a man killed by a snake, 2007
Pencil drawing on assembled sheets of paper, hair, 30 x 40 cm
Collection Isabelle Alfonsi

Black Maria (Phenomena Overwhelming Consciousness), 2008
Installation with eleven pigment prints on archival rag paper (60 x 80 cm) and 12 black and white slides, dimensions variable
Digital print: Studio Franck Bordas
Collection Ginette Moulin & Guillaume Houzé, Paris; Collection Béatrice Chassepot
Exhibition view and production: Centre d'art contemporain de la Ferme du Buisson, Noisiel
Photo: Nicolas Prache

p. 9
Matrix for the series of *Moulage sur le vif (Vide-poches)*, 2009
Scan, 150 x 230 cm
Scan: Studio Franck Bordas

p. 10
Premier rêve d'Oskar Fischinger, 2008
Two 16mm films transferred to HD, color, silent, 1'48 & 1'30
Exhibition view, musée d'Art moderne de la Ville de Paris, 2009
Collection musée d'Art moderne de la Ville de Paris

p. 11
Exhibition view, galerie Balice Hertling, Paris, 2010
With *Homonymes*; *Film-Lampe*; *De l'argent filmé de profil et de trois-quarts*, and *Floues et colorées*, 2010
Photo: François Doury

p. 13
Savane autour de Bangui et le fleuve Utubangui, 2003–2007
Twelve pigment prints on archival rag paper, 50 x 35.5 cm each
Digital print: Studio Franck Bordas
Collection Fonds national d'art contemporain, Paris

p. 14–15
Paysage avec poussin et témoins oculaires (Version I), 2008
Plywood plinths and panels, various objects, circa 500 x 800 cm, maximum height: 305 cm
Exhibition view, Kunstverein Düsseldorf, Dusseldorf, 2009
Photo: Martin Pfeifle
Collection Frac Aquitaine, Bordeaux

p. 16–17, 18, 19
Paysage avec poussin et témoins oculaires (Version IV), 2011
Installation view and details
Plinths and picture rails in concrete-covered plywood, various aluminum and wood objects, circa 400 x 700 cm, maximum height: 260 cm
Exhibition view, 1m3, Lausanne, 2011
Photo: Josef Hannibal
Collection Stéphane Ribordy, Geneva

p. 21
Film-Lampe, 2010
16mm film transferred to HD, color, silent, 1'25
Camera: Thomas Brésard, Jérôme Javelle
Collection Galleria d'Arte Moderna e Contemporanea (GAMeC), Bergamo

p. 22
De l'argent filmé de profil et de trois-quarts, 2010
16mm film transferred to HD, color, silent, 1'58
Camera: Thomas Brésard, Jérôme Javelle

p. 23
Floues et colorées, 2010
16mm film transferred to HD, color, silent, 3'12
Camera: Thomas Brésard, Jérôme Javelle

p. 24–25
View of the exhibition *Monsieur Miroir*, Fondation d'Entreprise Ricard, Paris, 2010
Background: *Impressions*, 2010
Wall spray paintings, dimensions variable
Realization: Thibaut Lenzinger
Foreground: *Homonymes*, 2010
Photo: Florian Kleinefenn/Fondation d'entreprise Ricard

p. 26–27
Homonymes, 2010
Hard, colored plaster cast, 120 x 60 cm, maximum height: 35 cm
Photo: François Doury
Collection Tony Salamé, Beyrouth

p. 28, 29, 30
Homonymes, 2010, details
Hard, colored plaster cast, 120 x 60 cm, maximum height: 35 cm
Cast: Pierre Imbertèche
Photo: François Doury

p. 35
Le Parc de Sans-Souci, détail, 2005
Assembled sheets of paper, hair, 38 x 28 cm
Collection of the artist

p. 36, 37
Bons à tirer, 2008
Ten pigment prints on archival rag paper, 30 x 40 cm
Digital print: Studio Franck Bordas
p. 36: Collection Clément Dirié

p. 38, 39, 40, 41
Black Maria (Phenomena Overwhelming Consciousness), 2008
11 drawings and 12 photographs
Book, 20 x 25 cm, black and white, 24 pages, published by the Studio Luc Derycke, Ghent
Produced by the Parc culturel de Rentilly
Photo: Isabelle Cornaro and Nicolas Prache
Model: Alix Dionot-Morani

p. 43
Cinésculptures (Polyèdres), 2008
Eight pigment prints on archival rag paper, 50 x 35 cm
Photo: Nicolas Prache
Digital print: Studio Franck Bordas

p. 44–45, 46
Du cinématique, 2011
Eight hard, colored plaster casts, 100 x 130 x 20 cm each
Five black & white spray paintings on paper, 170 x 130 cm each
One black & white wall spray painting, 340 x 260 cm
View of the exhibition *Un'Espressione Geografica. Unità eldentità dell'Italia attraverso l'Arte Contemporanea*, Fondazione Sandretto re Rebaudengo, Turin, Italy, 2011
Photo: Maurizio Elia

p. 48, 49
Le Proche et le lointain, 2011
Installation view and details
Six showcases with colored paper and various objects, circa 700 x 700 cm, height variable
Exhibition view, Collège des Bernardins, Paris, 2011
p. 51
View of the exhibition *Unto This Last*, Raven Row, London, 2010
Moulage sur le vif (Vide-poches), 2009
Pigment print on archival rag paper, 50 x 180 cm
Digital print: Studio Franck Bordas
p. 52, 53, 54, 55
Premier rêve d'Oskar Fischinger, 2008
Two 16mm films transferred to HD, color, mute, 1'48 and 1'30
Collection musée d'Art moderne de la Ville de Paris
p. 56, 57
Le Proche et le lointain, 2011, details
Six showcases with colored paper and various objects, circa 700 x 700 cm
p. 58
Moulage sur le vif (Vide-poches), 2011
Pigment print on archival rag paper, 70 x 100 cm
Digital print: Studio Franck Bordas
p. 60
Vanité à vif, 2001
Super 8 film transferred to HD, color, sound, 3'10
Camera: Gilles-Antoine Langlois
Collection Flavio Albanese
p. 64
Moulage sur le vif (Vide-poches), 2011
Pigment print on archival rag paper, 20 x 30 cm
Digital print: Studio Franck Bordas

Biography

Solo* and Group** Exhibition (Selection)

Born in 1974, Isabelle Cornaro lives and works in Paris.

She graduated from the Ecole nationale supérieure des Beaux-Arts in Paris. She held residencies at the Pavillon/Palais de Tokyo in 2006, at the Parc culturel de Rentilly in 2007, and at the Ateliers new-yorkais/ISCP, New York, in 2010.

Between 2006 and 2009 she published three artist's books: *De l'adresse* and *Black Maria*, MER/Luc Derycke, Ghent; *Plinths Arrangements*, Laboratoire de Recherche du Pavillon, Paris.

Her work features among the following public collections: Centre Pompidou, Musée national d'Art moderne, Paris; Fonds national d'Art contemporain, Paris; Fonds municipal d'Art contemporain, Paris; Musée d'Art moderne de la Ville de Paris, Paris; Frac Île-de-France, Paris; Frac Aquitaine, Bordeaux; GAMeC, Bergamo.

She is represented by the Galerie Balice Hertling, Paris.
www.balicehertling.com

Exhibitions

* 2013
Kunsthalle Bern, Bern

* 2012
Le Magasin, Grenoble
Frac Aquitaine, Bordeaux

* 2011
Le Proche et le lointain, Collège des Bernardins, Paris
Du Cinématique, 1m3, Lausanne

* 2010
Homonymes, Gallerie Balice Hertling, Paris
Passages – Centre d'Art Contemporain, Troyes

* 2009
Kunstverein Düsseldorf, Düsseldorf

* 2008
Orion Aveugle, récits avec figures projetées, Centre d'art contemporain de la Ferme du Buisson, Noisiel
Parc culturel de Rentilly, Rentilly

**2011
Un'Espressione Geografica, Fondazione Sandretto Re Rebaudengo, Turin
Living Room Exotica, Kunsthaus Glarus, Glarus
Extra-city, Antwerp
Vide-poches, SculptureCenter, New York

**2010
Monsieur Miroir, 12e Prix Ricard, Fondation d'entreprise Ricard, Paris
L'Ipotesi del Cristallo, GAMeC, Bergamo
La Vie saisie par l'art, CAPC, Bordeaux
Unto This Last, Raven Row, London
Prisonniers du Soleil, Le Plateau – Frac Île-de-France, Paris

**2009
Le Travail de Rivière, Le Crédac, Ivry
Three Black Minutes, Künstlerhaus, Stuttgart

Colophon

Editor
Clément Dirié
Copy editor
Clare Manchester
Translations from the French
Deke Dusinberre (Alice Motard, Clément Dirié)
Design
Gavillet & Rust, Geneva
Cover
Moulage sur le vif (Vide-poches), 2011
Color Separation and Print
Musumeci S.p.A., Quart (Aosta)
Typeface
Hermes-Sans (www.optimo.ch)

This book has been published with the support of the Centre national des arts plastiques.

This book is published on the occasion of:

the presentation of the work *Paysage avec poussin et témoins oculaires (Version III)* at the Centre Pompidou in 2011-2012—Isabelle Cornaro was awarded the 12th Prix Fondation d'entreprise Ricard

Fondation d'entreprise Ricard
12, rue Boissy d'Anglas
75008 Paris – France
www.fondation-entreprise-ricard.com

the solo exhibition at Le Magasin, Grenoble, from June 2 through September 2, 2012

Le Magasin – Centre National d'Art Contemporain
Director: Yves Aupetitallot
155, Cours Berriat –
Site Bouchayer-Viallet
38000 Grenoble – France
www.magasin-cnac.org

With the support of Ministère de la Culture et de la Communication – Direction Régionale des Affaires Culturelles Rhône-Alpes, Région Rhône-Alpes, Département de l'Isère, and Ville de Grenoble

the solo exhibition at Kunsthalle Bern, Spring 2013

Kunsthalle Bern
Director: Fabrice Stroun
Helvetiaplatz 1CH-3005 Bern
T + 41 31 350 00 43
F + 41 31 350 00 41
www.kunsthalle-bern.ch

The Kunsthalle Bern wishes to thank Kultur Stadt Bern for their generous support

This publication received the support of:
Centre d'art contemporain / Passages
9, rue Jeanne d'Arc, 10000 Troyes – France
www.cac-passages.fr
Communauté d'Agglomération de Marne-et-Gondoire / Parc culturel de Rentilly
President: Michel Chartier – Director: Armelle Thévenot
1, rue de l'étang, 77600 Bussy-Saint-Martin – France
www.parcculturelrentilly.fr
as well as of
Galerie Balice Hertling
47, rue Ramponneau, 75020 Paris – France
www.balicehertling.com

Printed in Europe

Published by
JRP|Ringier
Letzigraben 134
CH-8047 Zurich
T +41 (0) 43 311 27 50
F +41 (0) 43 311 27 51
E info@jrp-ringier.com
www.jrp-ringier.com

ISBN 978-3-03764-208-5
(French edition available: ISBN 978-3-03764-209-2)

JRP|Ringier books are available internationally at selected bookstores and from the following distribution partners:

Switzerland
AVA Verlagsauslieferung AG
Centralweg 16
CH-8910 Affoltern a.A.
verlagsservice@ava.ch, www.ava.ch

France
Les presses du réel
35 rue Colson
F-21000 Dijon
info@lespressesdureel.com
www.lespressesdureel.com

Germany and Austria
Vice Versa Vertrieb
Immanuelkirchstrasse 12
D-10405 Berlin
info@vice-versa-vertrieb.de
www.vice-versa-vertrieb.de

UK and other European countries
Cornerhouse Publications
70 Oxford Street
UK-Manchester M1 5NH
publications@cornerhouse.org
www.cornerhouse.org/books

USA, Canada, Asia, and Australia
ARTBOOK|D.A.P.
155 Sixth Avenue, 2nd Floor
USA-New York, NY 10013
dap@dapinc.com, www.artbook.com

For a list of our partner bookshops or for any general questions, please contact JRP|Ringier directly at info@jrp-ringier.com, or visit our homepage www.jrp-ringier.com for further information about our program.

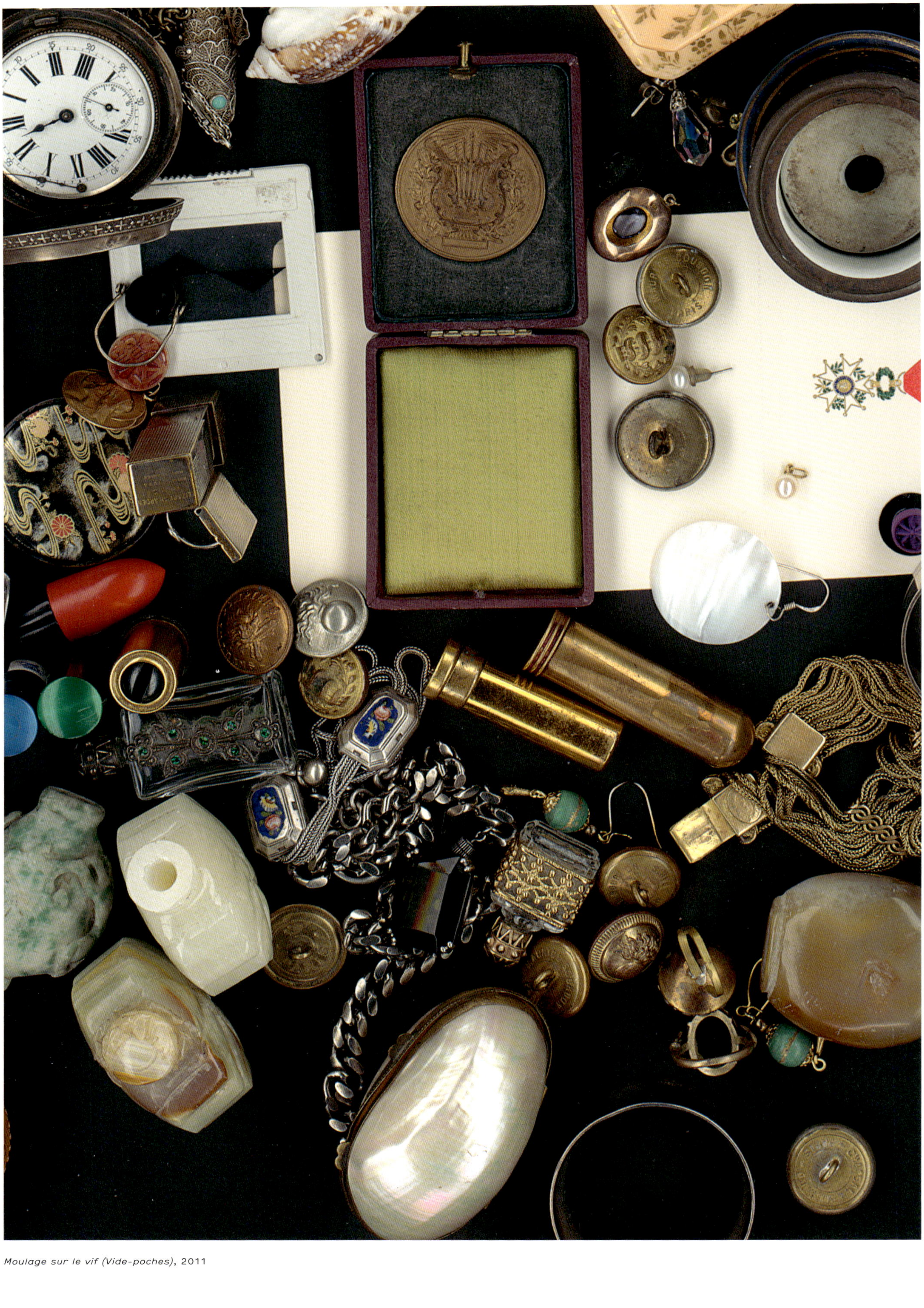

Moulage sur le vif (Vide-poches), 2011